Guitar Chord Songbook

Two-Chord Songs

ISBN 978-1-4803-4207-1

7777 W. Bluemound Rd. P.O. Box 13819 Milwaukee, WI 53213

Visit Hal Leonard Online at
www.halleonard.com

Contents

ABC

Words and Music by
Alphonso Mizell, Frederick Perren,
Deke Richards and Berry Gordy

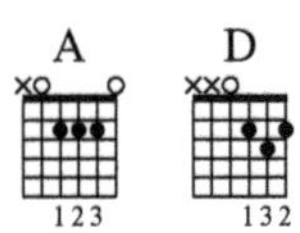

Intro | A D | A D |

Verse 1

```
    A            D
You went to school to learn girl,
           A                   D
Things you never, never knew be - fore.
   A           D
Like I before E ex - cept after C.
       A               D
And why two plus two makes four.
               A                           D
Now, now, now, I'm going to teach you. (Teach you, teach you.)
A                D
All about love, dear. (All about love.)
A              D
Sit yourself down, take a seat
A                D
All you gotta do is re - peat after me.
```

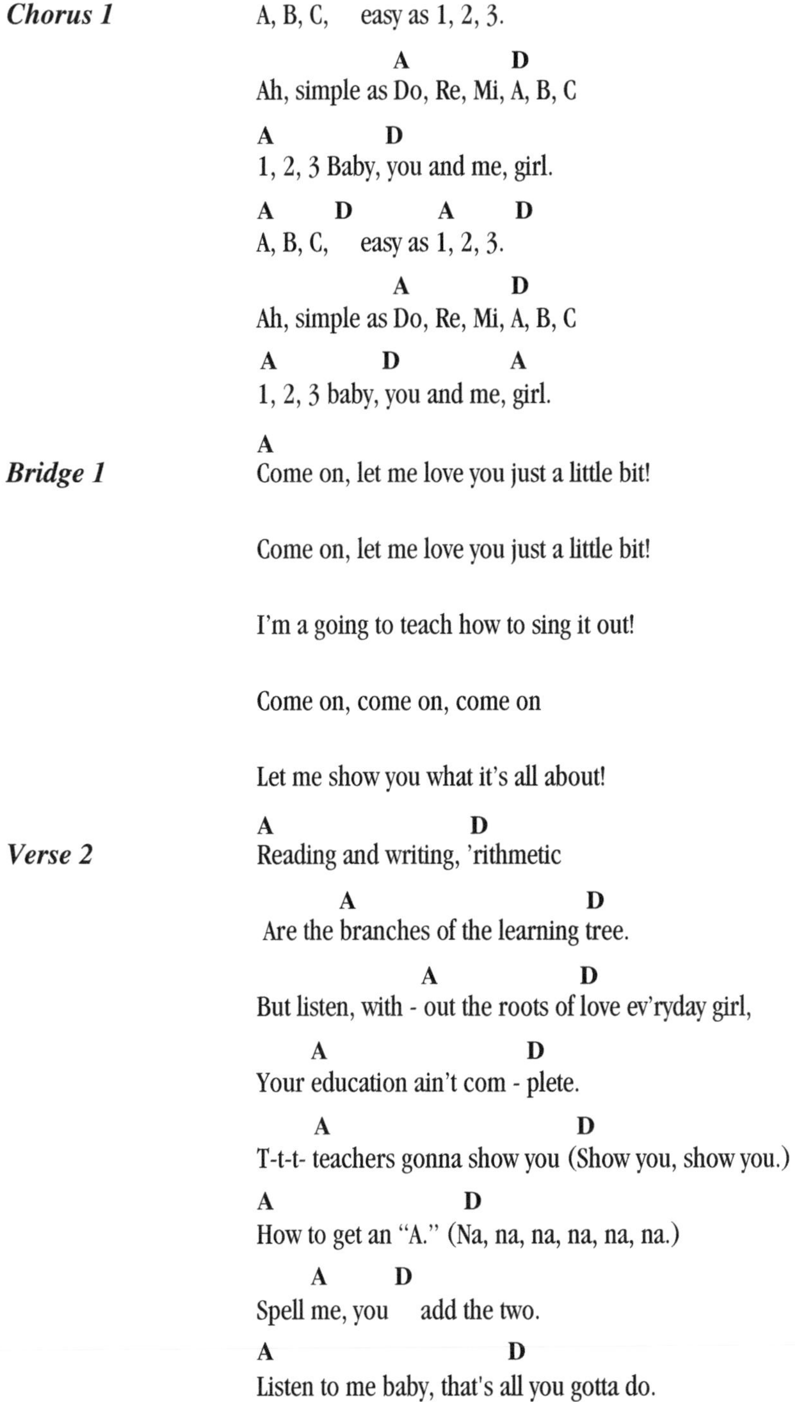

Chorus 1

A D A D
A, B, C, easy as 1, 2, 3.

A D
Ah, simple as Do, Re, Mi, A, B, C

A D
1, 2, 3 Baby, you and me, girl.

A D A D
A, B, C, easy as 1, 2, 3.

A D
Ah, simple as Do, Re, Mi, A, B, C

A D A
1, 2, 3 baby, you and me, girl.

Bridge 1

A
Come on, let me love you just a little bit!

Come on, let me love you just a little bit!

I'm a going to teach how to sing it out!

Come on, come on, come on

Let me show you what it's all about!

Verse 2

A D
Reading and writing, 'rithmetic

A D
Are the branches of the learning tree.

A D
But listen, with - out the roots of love ev'ryday girl,

A D
Your education ain't com - plete.

A D
T-t-t- teachers gonna show you (Show you, show you.)

A D
How to get an "A." (Na, na, na, na, na, na.)

A D
Spell me, you add the two.

A D
Listen to me baby, that's all you gotta do.

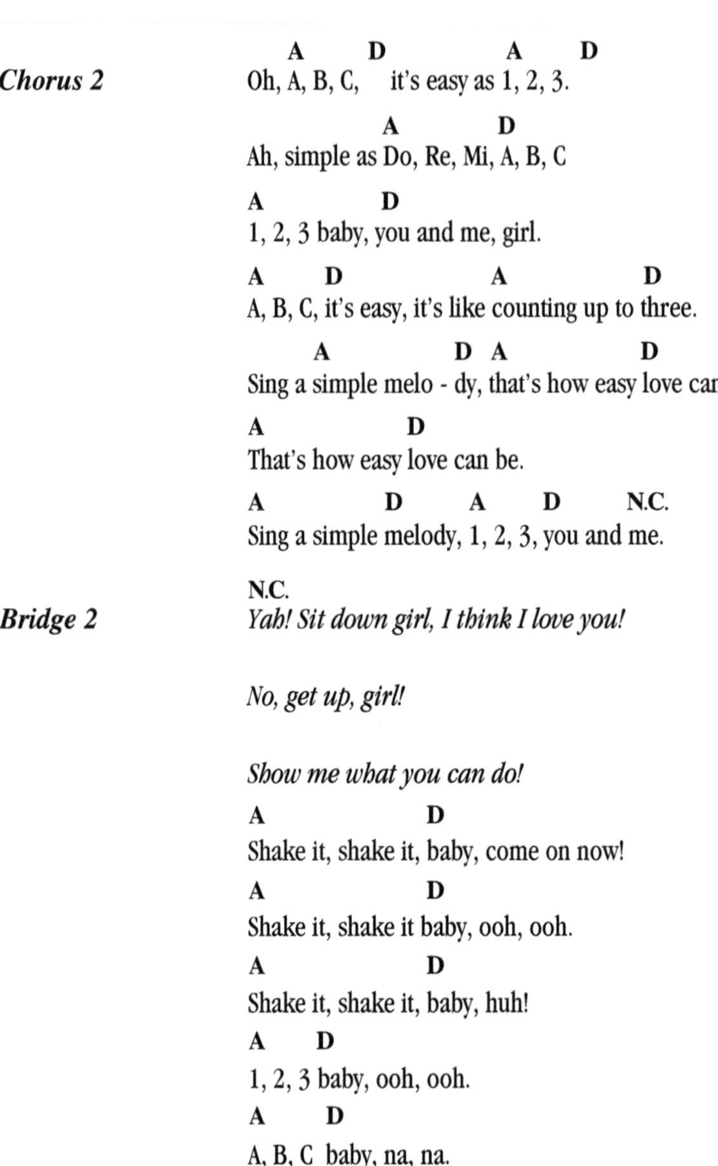

Chorus 2

A D A D
Oh, A, B, C, it's easy as 1, 2, 3.

A D
Ah, simple as Do, Re, Mi, A, B, C

A D
1, 2, 3 baby, you and me, girl.

A D A D
A, B, C, it's easy, it's like counting up to three.

A D A D
Sing a simple melo - dy, that's how easy love can be.

A D
That's how easy love can be.

A D A D N.C.
Sing a simple melody, 1, 2, 3, you and me.

Bridge 2

N.C.
Yah! Sit down girl, I think I love you!

No, get up, girl!

Show me what you can do!

A D
Shake it, shake it, baby, come on now!

A D
Shake it, shake it baby, ooh, ooh.

A D
Shake it, shake it, baby, huh!

A D
1, 2, 3 baby, ooh, ooh.

A D
A, B, C baby, na, na.

A D
Do, re, mi baby, huh!

A D
That's how easy love can be.

```
             A        D          A          D
Chorus 3     A, B, C, it's easy, it's like counting up to three.

                 A          D A            D      A
             Sing a simple melo - dy,  that's how easy love can be.

             I'm a gonna teach you how to sing it out.

             Come-a, come-a, come-a, let me show you what it's all about.
             A        D          A          D
             A, B, C, it's easy, it's like counting up to three.
                 A          D A            D      A
             Sing a simple melo - dy,  that's how easy love can be.

             I'm a gonna teach you how to sing it out,

             Sing it out, sing it out, baby, baby.
```

Outro *Repeat Chorus 3 till fade*

Achy Breaky Heart

(Don't Tell My Heart)

Words and Music by
Don Von Tress

Melody:

You can tell the world you never was my girl.

A E

Intro | A | | | |

Verse 1

A
You can tell the world you never was my girl.
E
You can burn my clothes when I'm gone.

Or you can tell your friends just what a fool I've been
A
And laugh and joke about me on the phone.

You can tell my arms go back on to the farm.
E
You can tell my feet to hit the floor.

Or you can tell my lips to tell my fingertips
A
They won't be reachin' out for you no more.

Chorus 1

A
Don't tell my heart, my achy, breaky heart.
E
I just don't think he'd under - stand.

And if you tell my heart, my achy, breaky heart,
A
He might blow up and kill this man. Ooh.

Interlude 1 | A | | | E |
| | | | A |

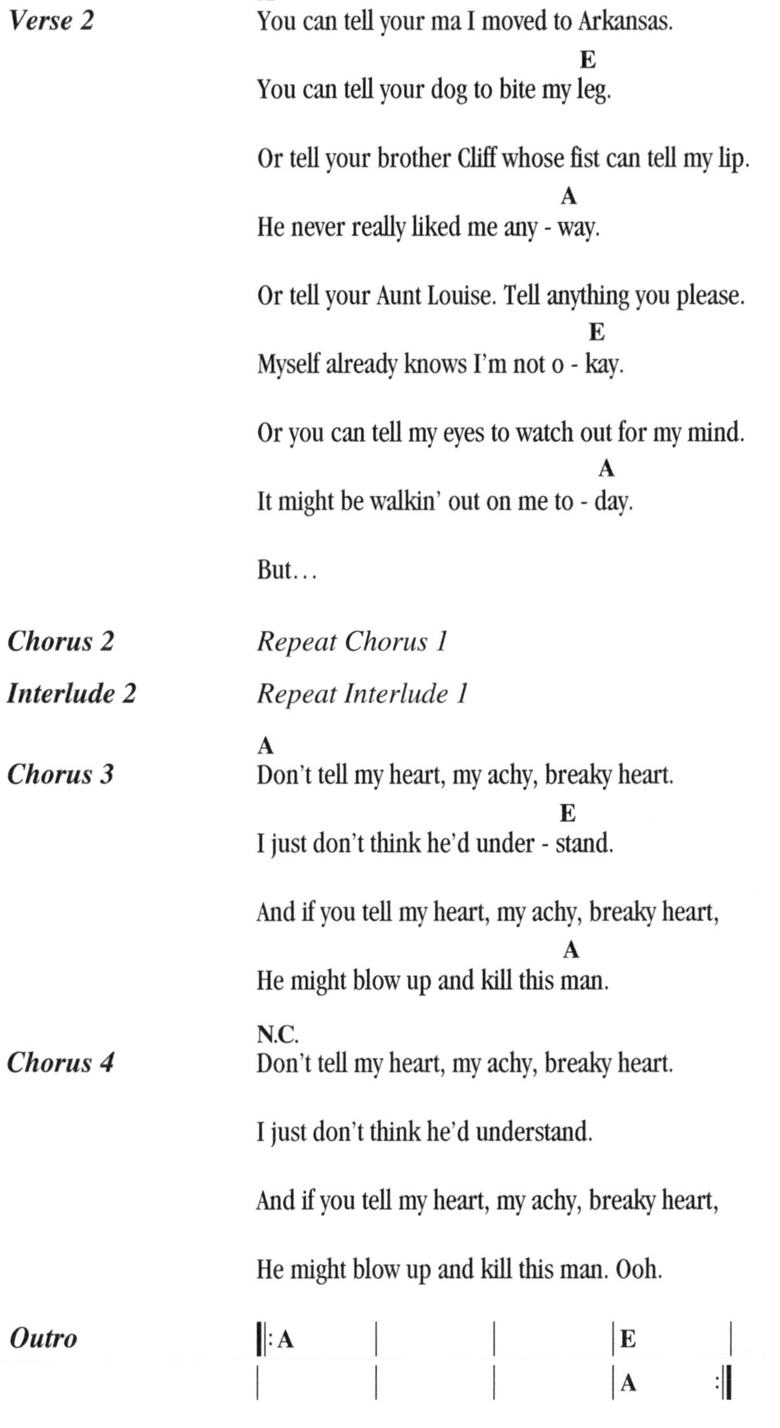

Verse 2

A
You can tell your ma I moved to Arkansas.
E
You can tell your dog to bite my leg.

Or tell your brother Cliff whose fist can tell my lip.
A
He never really liked me any - way.

Or tell your Aunt Louise. Tell anything you please.
E
Myself already knows I'm not o - kay.

Or you can tell my eyes to watch out for my mind.
A
It might be walkin' out on me to - day.

But...

Chorus 2 — *Repeat Chorus 1*

Interlude 2 — *Repeat Interlude 1*

Chorus 3

A
Don't tell my heart, my achy, breaky heart.
E
I just don't think he'd under - stand.

And if you tell my heart, my achy, breaky heart,
A
He might blow up and kill this man.

Chorus 4

N.C.
Don't tell my heart, my achy, breaky heart.

I just don't think he'd understand.

And if you tell my heart, my achy, breaky heart,

He might blow up and kill this man. Ooh.

Outro

‖: **A** | | | **E** |
| | | **A** :‖

Anyone Else but You

from the Motion Picture Soundtrack JUNO

Words and Music by
Kimya Dawson and Adam Green

Melody:
You're a part-time lov-er and a

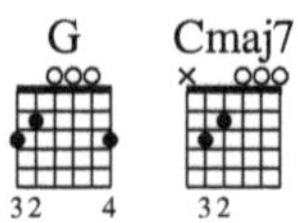

G
Cmaj7
32 4
32

Intro ‖: G | | Cmaj7 | :‖

Verse 1

```
              G
Male: You're a part-time lover and a full-time friend.
    Cmaj7
The monkey on your back is the latest trend.
 G                                      Cmaj7
I don't see what anyone can see in anyone else but you.
         G
Female: Here is the church and here is the steeple.
   Cmaj7
We sure are cute for two ugly people.
 G                                      Cmaj7
I don't see what anyone can see in anyone ___ else but you.
```

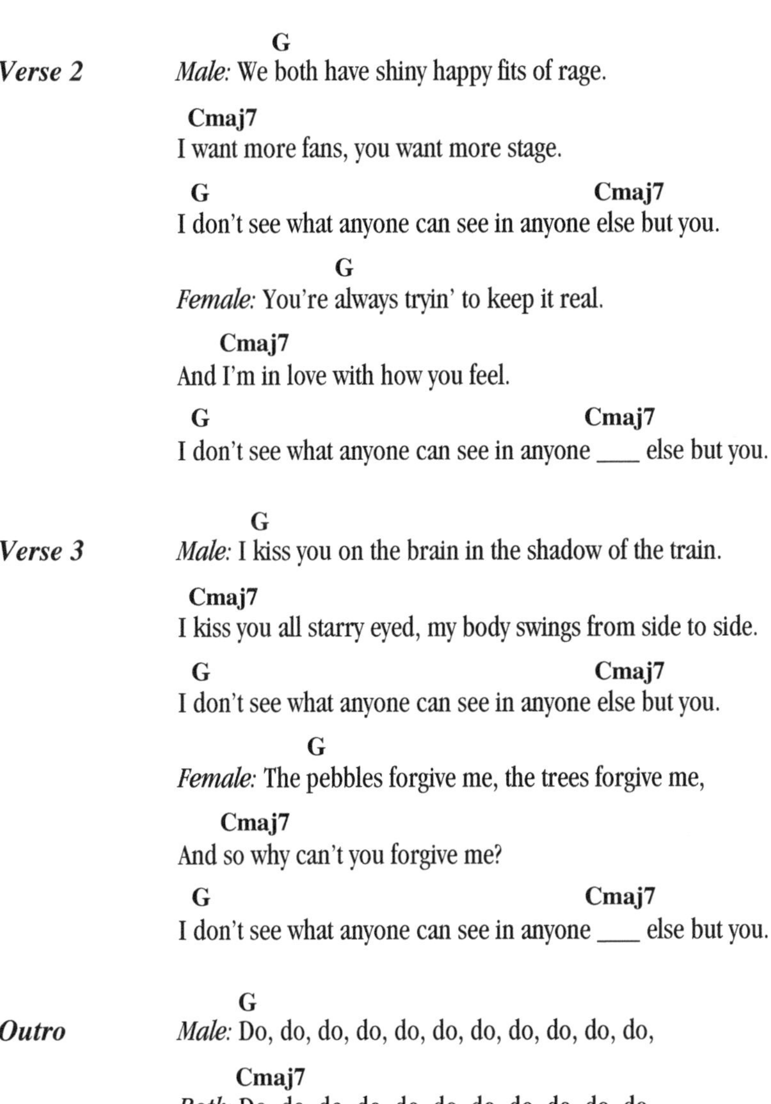

Verse 2

G
Male: We both have shiny happy fits of rage.

Cmaj7
I want more fans, you want more stage.

G **Cmaj7**
I don't see what anyone can see in anyone else but you.

G
Female: You're always tryin' to keep it real.

Cmaj7
And I'm in love with how you feel.

G **Cmaj7**
I don't see what anyone can see in anyone ___ else but you.

Verse 3

G
Male: I kiss you on the brain in the shadow of the train.

Cmaj7
I kiss you all starry eyed, my body swings from side to side.

G **Cmaj7**
I don't see what anyone can see in anyone else but you.

G
Female: The pebbles forgive me, the trees forgive me,

Cmaj7
And so why can't you forgive me?

G **Cmaj7**
I don't see what anyone can see in anyone ___ else but you.

Outro

G
Male: Do, do, do, do, do, do, do, do, do, do, do,

Cmaj7
Both: Do, do, do, do, do, do, do, do, do, do, do.

G **Cmaj7 G**
I don't see what anyone can see in anyone else but you.

Bo Diddley

Words and Music by Ellas McDaniel

(Capo 3rd fret)

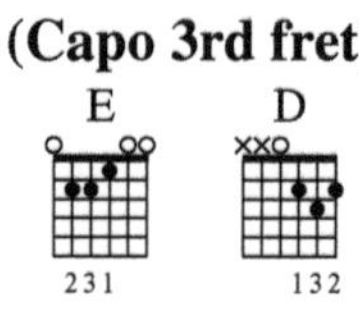

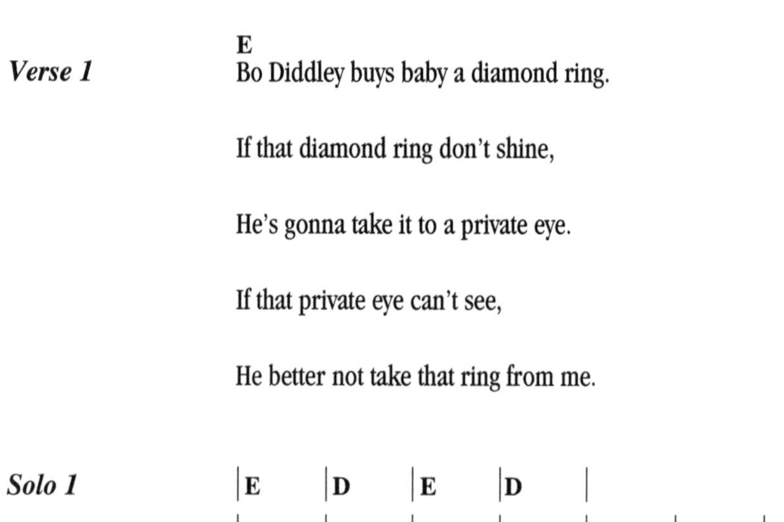

Intro	‖: **E**		:‖ ***Play 4 times***

Verse 1

E
Bo Diddley buys baby a diamond ring.

If that diamond ring don't shine,

He's gonna take it to a private eye.

If that private eye can't see,

He better not take that ring from me.

Solo 1

E	**D**	**E**	**D**		
E					

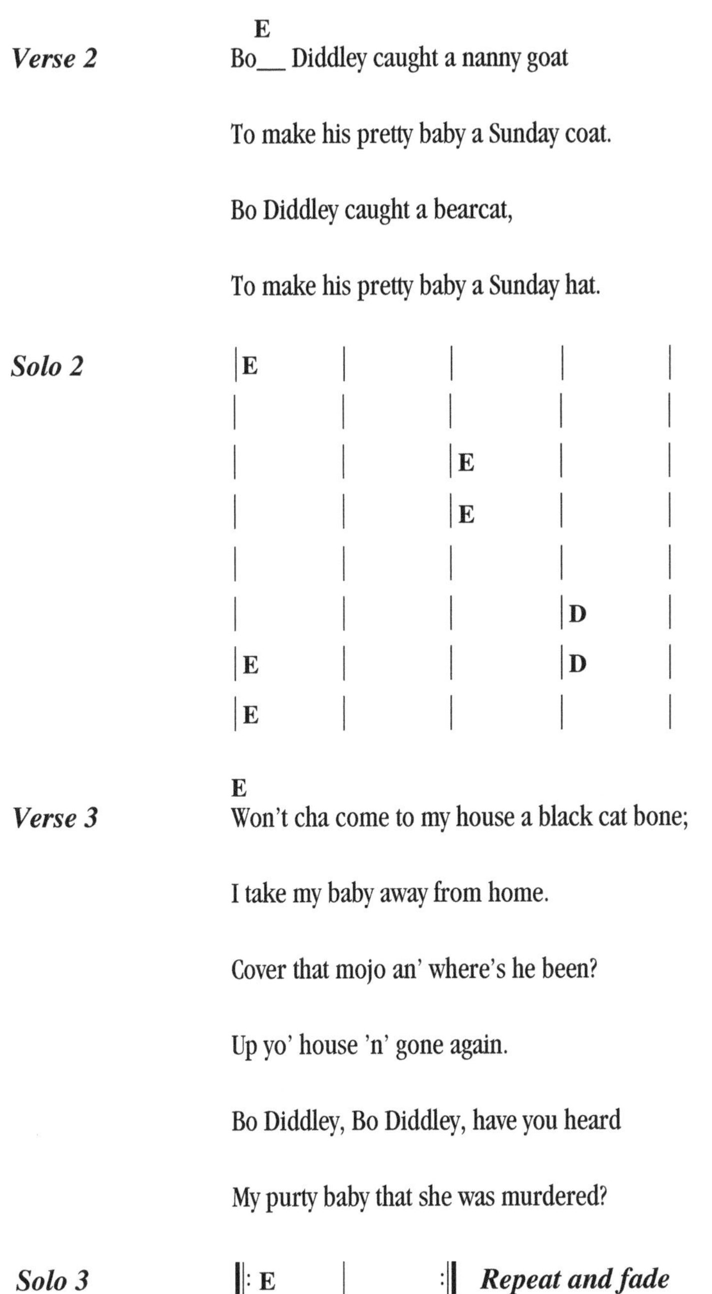

Verse 2

E
Bo__ Diddley caught a nanny goat

To make his pretty baby a Sunday coat.

Bo Diddley caught a bearcat,

To make his pretty baby a Sunday hat.

Solo 2

E				
		E		
		E		
			D	
E			D	
E				

Verse 3

E
Won't cha come to my house a black cat bone;

I take my baby away from home.

Cover that mojo an' where's he been?

Up yo' house 'n' gone again.

Bo Diddley, Bo Diddley, have you heard

My purty baby that she was murdered?

Solo 3

‖: **E** | :‖ ***Repeat and fade***

Brick House

Words and Music by Lionel Richie,
Ronald LaPread, Walter Orange,
Milan Williams, Thomas McClary
and William King

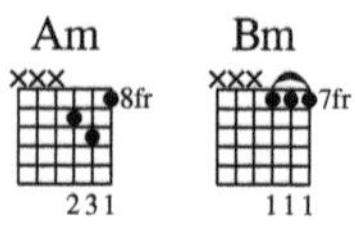

Chorus 1

```
                Am  Bm  Am      Bm  Am
Ow, she's a brick           house.
Am             Bm       Am
   She's might - y, might - y
                     Bm     Am
Just lettin' it all hang ___ out.
               Am  Bm  Am      Bm  Am
Ah, she's a brick          house.
       Am             Bm           Am
I like ladies stacked and that's a fact.

Ain't holdin' nothin' back.
Bm  Am             Bm  Am
Ow,  she's a brick        house.
Bm  Am                          Bm        Am
             Well, we're together ev'rybody knows
                       Bm     Am
This is how the sto - ry goes.
```

Verse 1

Am
She knows she's got

Ev'ry - thing

Mm, that a woman needs

To get a man. Yeah, yeah.

How can she lose

With the stuff she use?

Thirty - six, twenty - four, thir - ty - six.

Ow, what a winning hand - ful.

Chorus 2

Am Bm Am Bm Am
She's a brick house.

Am Bm
She's might - y, mighty

Am Bm
Just lettin' it all hang out.

Am Bm Am Bm
Ah, she's a brick house.

Am Bm Am
Oh, I like ladies stacked and that's a fact.

Bm
Ain't holdin' noth - in' back.

Am Bm Am
Oh, ___ she's a brick house.

Bm Am Bm Am
Yeah, ___ she's the one, the on - ly one

Bm Am
Built like an Am - azon.

```
Verse 2        Am
               Mm, ___ the clothes she wear,

               Her sex - y ways

                  Make an old man wish

                  For younger days yeah, yeah.

                  She knows she's built

               And knows how to please.

                  Sure 'nough can knock  a

               Strong man to his knees.

Chorus 3       Am                     Bm  Am        Bm  Am
               'Cause she's a brick           house.
               Am                   Bm       Am
               Yeah, she's might - y, mighty
                              Bm
               Just lettin' it all hang out.
               Am          Bm  Am        Bm  Am
               Hey,   brick          house.
                     Am             Bm               Am
               I like ladies stacked    and that's a fact.
                                    Bm          Am
               Ain't holdin' noth - in' back. Ow.
```

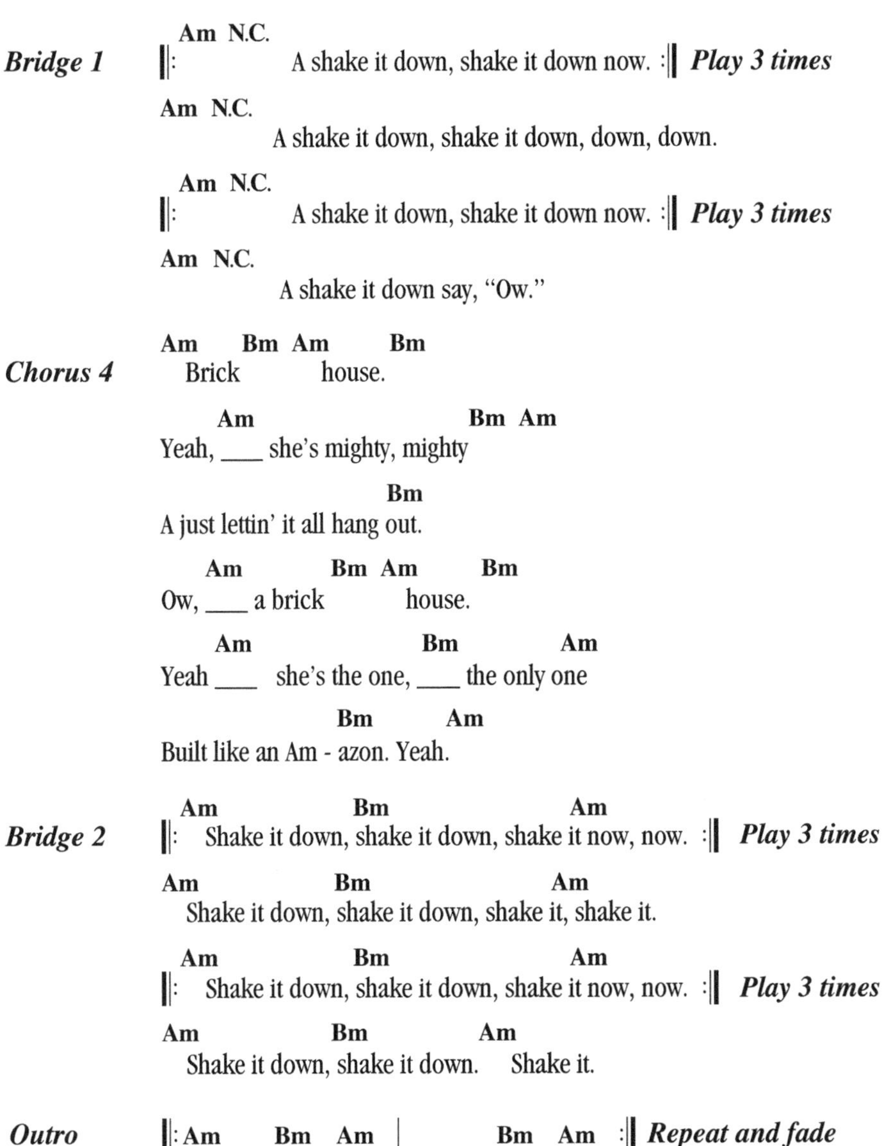
Bridge 1
Am N.C.
‖: A shake it down, shake it down now. :‖ Play 3 times
Am N.C.
A shake it down, shake it down, down, down.
Am N.C.
‖: A shake it down, shake it down now. :‖ Play 3 times
Am N.C.
A shake it down say, "Ow."
Chorus 4
Am Bm Am Bm
Brick house.
Am Bm Am
Yeah, ___ she's mighty, mighty
Bm
A just lettin' it all hang out.
Am Bm Am Bm
Ow, ___ a brick house.
Am Bm Am
Yeah ___ she's the one, ___ the only one
Bm Am
Built like an Am - azon. Yeah.
Bridge 2
Am Bm Am
‖: Shake it down, shake it down, shake it now, now. :‖ Play 3 times
Am Bm Am
Shake it down, shake it down, shake it, shake it.
Am Bm Am
‖: Shake it down, shake it down, shake it now, now. :‖ Play 3 times
Am Bm Am
Shake it down, shake it down. Shake it.
Outro
‖: Am Bm Am | Bm Am :‖ Repeat and fade

Day-O
(The Banana Boat Song)

Words and Music by
Irving Burgie and William Attaway

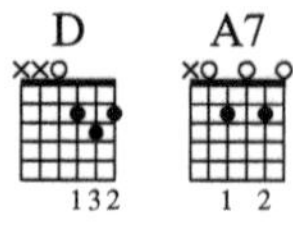

Chorus 1

```
N.C.
Day-o, day-o. Daylight come and me wan' go home.

Day, me say day, me say day, me say day,

Me say day, me say day-o.

Daylight come and me wan' go home.
```

Verse 1

```
D
Work all night on a drink of rum.
                        A7      D
Daylight come and me wan' go home.

Stack banana till de morning come.
                        A7      D
Daylight come and me wan' go home.
```

Verse 2

```
D                          A7
Come, Mister tally man, tally me banana.
D                       A7      D
Daylight come and me wan' go home.
                           A7
Come, Mister tally man, tally me banana.
D                       A7      D
Daylight come and me wan' go home.
```

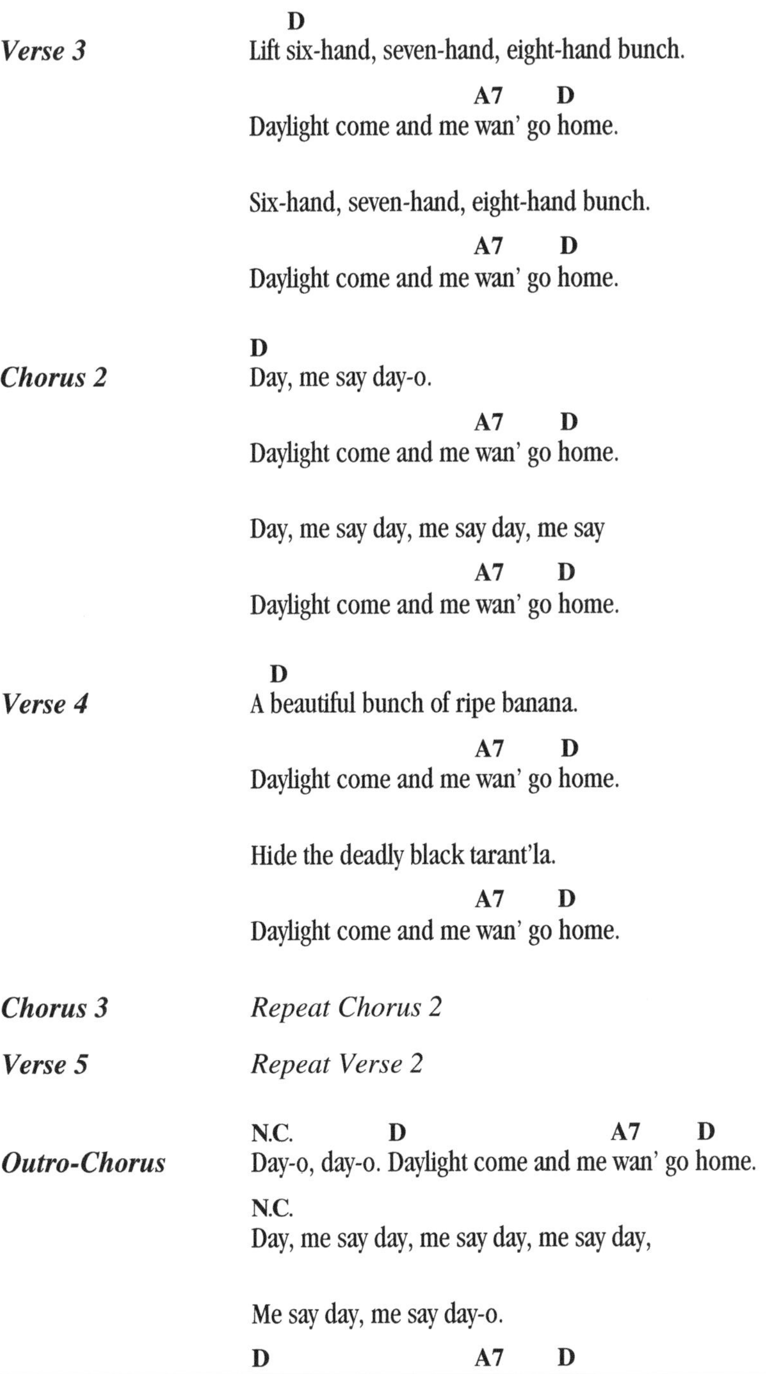

Verse 3

```
      D
Lift six-hand, seven-hand, eight-hand bunch.
                        A7       D
Daylight come and me wan' go home.

Six-hand, seven-hand, eight-hand bunch.
                        A7       D
Daylight come and me wan' go home.
```

Chorus 2

```
D
Day, me say day-o.
                        A7       D
Daylight come and me wan' go home.

Day, me say day, me say day, me say
                        A7       D
Daylight come and me wan' go home.
```

Verse 4

```
  D
A beautiful bunch of ripe banana.
                        A7       D
Daylight come and me wan' go home.

Hide the deadly black tarant'la.
                        A7       D
Daylight come and me wan' go home.
```

Chorus 3 *Repeat Chorus 2*

Verse 5 *Repeat Verse 2*

Outro-Chorus

```
N.C.           D                        A7       D
Day-o, day-o. Daylight come and me wan' go home.
N.C.
Day, me say day, me say day, me say day,

Me say day, me say day-o.
D                       A7       D
Daylight come and me wan' go home.
```

Deep in the Heart of Texas

Words by June Hershey
Music by Don Swander

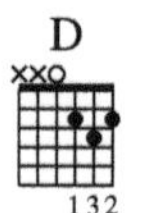

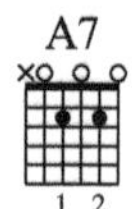

Verse 1

D
The stars at night are big and bright,

A7
(Deep in the heart of Texas.)

The prairie sky is wide and high,

D
(Deep in the heart of Texas.)

Verse 2

D
The sage in bloom is like perfume,

A7
(Deep in the heart of Texas.)

Reminds me of the one I love,

D
(Deep in the heart of Texas.)

Verse 3

D
The coyotes wail along the trail,

A7
(Deep in the heart of Texas.)

The rabbits rush around the brush,

D
(Deep in the heart of Texas.)

Verse 4

D
The cowboys cry, "Ki-yip-pee-yi,"

A7
(Deep in the heart of Texas.)

The doggies bawl, and bawl and bawl,

D
(Deep in the heart of Texas.)

Verse 5

D
The sage in bloom is like perfume,

A7
(Deep in the heart of Texas.)

Reminds me of the one I love,

D
(Deep in the heart of Texas.)

Outro

A7 D
‖: (Deep in the heart of Texas.) :‖ ***Repeat and fade***

Do the Funky Chicken

Words and Music by
Rufus Thomas

Melody:

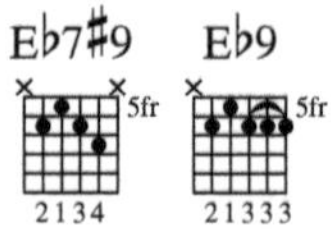

Intro

Eb7#9
Y'all come on in, now. Come right on down front.

I got somethin' I wanna show ya.

Now, y'all heard of "The Popcorn." Y'all heard of "The Dog."

And you heard about all them other dances.

But now there's a brand new dance that's goin' around.

I wanna show you exactly what I'm talkin' about.

I'm talkin' about "The Funky Chicken."

"Y'all ready?" (Yeah.) I said, "Y'all ready?" (Yeah.)

OK, here we go.

Verse 1

Eb7#9
You raise your left arm up, and your right arm too.

Let me tell ya just what to do.

Start both arms to flappin', start your feet to kickin'.

That's when you know, you're doin' the funky chicken. Oh, oh.

Interlude 1 | E♭9 | | | |

Second Spasm
E♭7♯9
You put both arms up across your face

Your knees start wigglin' all over the place.

You flap your arms and your feet start kickin'.

Then you know you're doin' the funky chicken. Oh, oh.

Interlude 2 *Repeat Interlude 1*

Breakdown
E♭7♯9
Oh, I'm feelin' it now. I feel so unnecessary.

This is the kidda, this is the kidda stuff,

That makes you feel like you wanna do somethin' nasty.

Like waste some chicken gravy on your white shirt.

Right down front. Here we go, y'all.

Verse 2
E♭7♯9
You work both arms and you work both feet.

You together, baby, you're right on the beat.

You flap your arms and your feet start kickin'.

Then you know you're doin' the funky chicken.
E♭9
Oh, oh it's alright.

Outro-Chorus
E♭9
‖: Do the funky chicken, now. :‖ ***Play 4 times***

‖: Do the funky chicken, now. Ha, ha, ha. :‖ ***Play 4 times***

Oh, oh, do the funky chicken, now. ***Fade out***

Dream Baby
(How Long Must I Dream)

Words and Music by
Cindy Walker

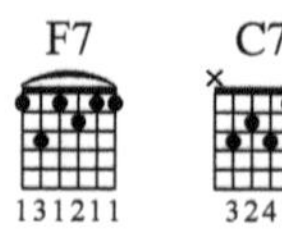

Intro ‖: **F7** | :‖ ***Play 4 times***

Chorus 1
C7
Sweet dream baby,
Sweet dream baby,
F7
Sweet dream baby,
C7 **F7**
How long must I dream?

Verse 1
C7
Dream baby, got me dreaming sweet dreams the whole day through.
Dream baby, got me dreaming sweet dreams, the nighttime too.
F7
I love you, and I'm dreamin' of you; but that won't do.
C7
Dream baby, you can stop my dreaming.
F7
You can make my dreams come true.

Chorus 2 *Repeat Chorus 1*

Verse 2 *Repeat Verse 1*

Chorus 3 *Repeat Chorus 1*

Outro *Repeat Chorus till fade*

Dreams

Words and Music by
Stevie Nicks

Melody:
Now, here you go a - gain. You say...

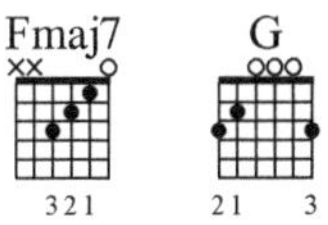
Fmaj7
G
321
21 3

Intro | **Fmaj7** | **G** | **Fmaj7** | **G** |

Verse 1

```
Fmaj7                 G
     Now, here you go__ again.
      Fmaj7                G
You say   you want your free - dom.
Fmaj7           G                         Fmaj7    G
     Well, who am I__ to keep you down?
Fmaj7           G
     It's only right__ that you should
Fmaj7               G
Play the way you feel__ it.
     Fmaj7         G                  Fmaj7
But listen carefully__ to the sound
              G
Of your lone - liness,
```

```
       Fmaj7                      G
Like a heartbeat, drives you mad,

          Fmaj7              G
In the still - ness of remem-bering

              Fmaj7   G                 Fmaj7   G
What you had             and what you lost,

                 Fmaj7   G                 Fmaj7    G
And what you had            and what you lost.
```

Chorus 1

```
     Fmaj7            G                      Fmaj7     G
Oh, thunder only hap - pens when it's rain - ing.

Fmaj7           G                            Fmaj7     G
Players only love__ you when they're play - ing.

     Fmaj7                  G                   Fmaj7     G
Say, women, they will come__ and they will go.

Fmaj7                G                        Fmaj7     G
When the rain washes__ you clean, you'll know.

      Fmaj7
You'll know.
```

Solo

```
|Fmaj7      |G          |        Fmaj7 |        |
|          G|           |        Fmaj7 |        |
```

```
         Fmaj7           G
Verse 2     Now, here I go__ again.

            Fmaj7          G
         I see    the crystal vis - ions.

         Fmaj7          G                 Fmaj7    G
            I keep my vis - ions to myself.

         Fmaj7         G
            It's only me__ who wants to

         Fmaj7                   G
         Wrap around your dreams.

            Fmaj7              G                    Fmaj7
         And have you any dreams__ you'd like to sell?

                       G              Fmaj7                   G
         Dreams of lone - liness, like a heartbeat, drives you mad,

                   Fmaj7           G
         In the still - ness of remem-bering

                        Fmaj7   G                 Fmaj7      G
         What you had              and what you lost

                           Fmaj7    G                 Fmaj7      G
         And what you had              and what you lost.
```

Chorus 2 ***Repeat Chorus 1***

```
         G            Fmaj7
Outro       You will know.

            G         Fmaj7
         Oh,__ you'll know.
```

Eleanor Rigby

Words and Music by John Lennon
and Paul McCartney

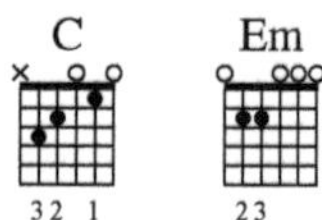

Intro

```
C                          Em
Ah, look at all the lonely people!
C                          Em
Ah, look at all the lonely people!
```

Verse 1

```
Em
Eleanor Rigby,
                                                  C
Picks up the rice in the church where a wedding has been,
              Em
Lives in a dream.

Waits at the window,
                                             C
Wearing a face that she keeps in a jar by the door,
          Em
Who is it for?
```

Chorus 1

```
Em
All the lonely people, where do they all come from?

All the lonely people, where do they all belong?
```

Verse 2

Em
Father McKenzie,

C (on "hear")
Writing the words of a sermon that no one will hear,

Em (on "near")
No one comes near.

Look at him working,

C (on "there")
Darning his socks in the night when there's nobody there,

Em (on "care")
What does he care?

Chorus 2 *Repeat Chorus 1*

Bridge

C **Em** (on "people")
Ah, look at all the lonely people!

C **Em** (on "people")
Ah, look at all the lonely people!

Verse 3

Em
Eleanor Rigby,

C (on "name")
Died in the church and was buried along with her name,

Em (on "came")
Nobody came.

Father McKenzie,

C (on "grave")
Wiping the dirt from his hands as he walks from the grave,

Em (on "saved")
No one was saved.

Chorus 3 *Repeat Chorus 1*

Feelin' Alright

Words and Music by
Dave Mason

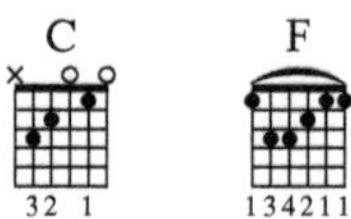

Verse 1

```
C                                    F
  It seems I've got to have a change of scene,
C                                       F
  'Cause ev'ry night I have the strangest dream.
C                               F
  Prisoned by the way it could have been.
C                                  F
  Left here on my own or so it seems.
C                                       F
  I've got to leave here 'fore I start to scream,
C                                                    F
  'Cause someone's locked the door and took the key.
```

Chorus 1

```
            C
You feelin' alright?
F                              C
  I'm not feelin' too good ___ myself.
F                   C
  Well, you feelin' alright?
F                              C           F
  I'm not feelin' too good ___ myself.
```

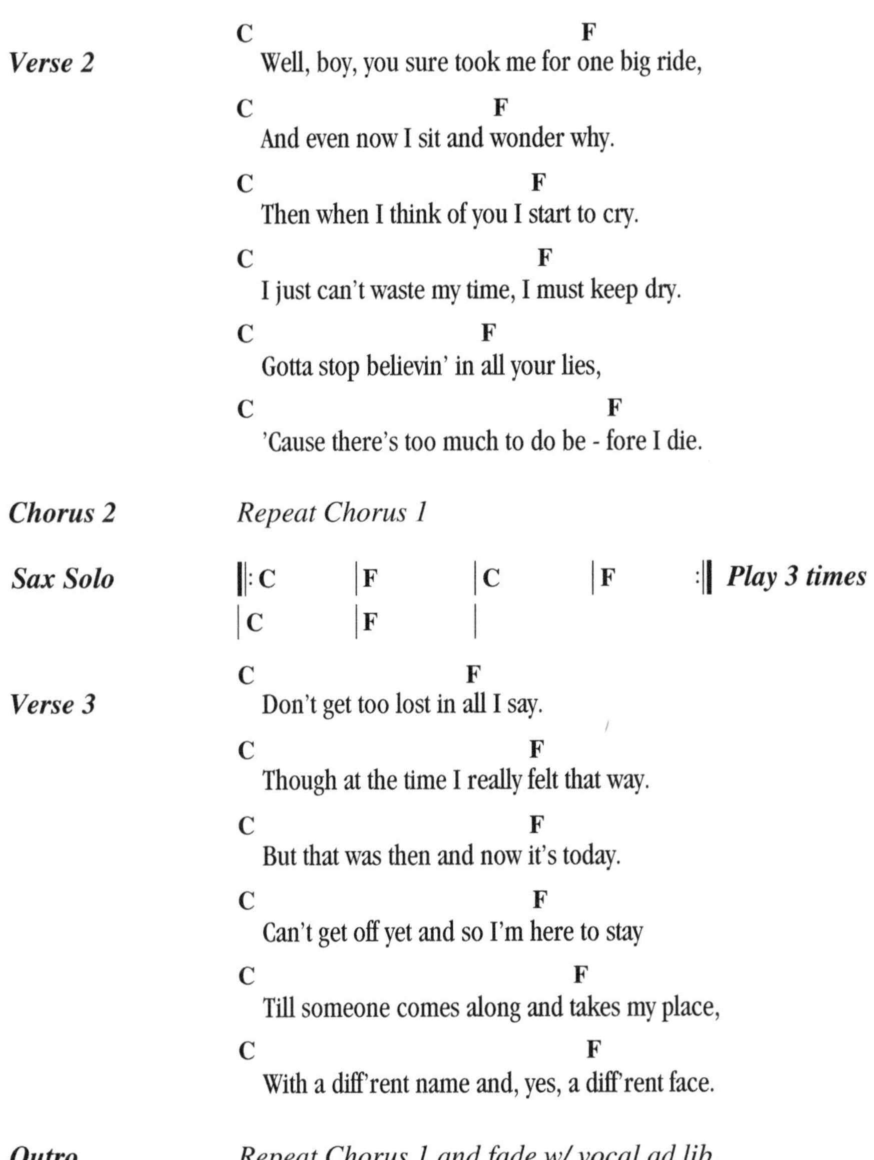

Verse 2

```
C                                       F
   Well, boy, you sure took me for one big ride,
C                              F
   And even now I sit and wonder why.
C                                  F
   Then when I think of you I start to cry.
C                                  F
   I just can't waste my time, I must keep dry.
C                            F
   Gotta stop believin' in all your lies,
C                                          F
   'Cause there's too much to do be - fore I die.
```

Chorus 2 *Repeat Chorus 1*

Sax Solo

```
||: C     | F     | C     | F     :|| Play 3 times
| C       | F     |
```

Verse 3

```
C                           F
   Don't get too lost in all I say.
C                                  F
   Though at the time I really felt that way.
C                                  F
   But that was then and now it's today.
C                                  F
   Can't get off yet and so I'm here to stay
C                                        F
   Till someone comes along and takes my place,
C                                         F
   With a diff'rent name and, yes, a diff'rent face.
```

Outro *Repeat Chorus 1 and fade w/ vocal ad lib.*

Fever

Words and Music by
John Davenport and Eddie Cooley

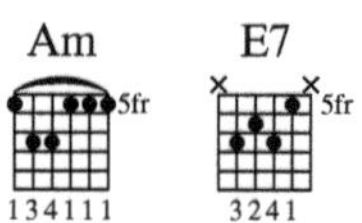

Intro ‖: **Am** | | **E7** | **Am** :‖

Verse 1

```
Am
   Never know how much I love you, never know how much I care.
                                        E7                    Am
When you put your arms around me, I get a fever that's so hard to bear.

You give me fever when you kiss me, fever when you hold me tight,
                   E7                    Am
Fever in the morning, fever all through the night.
```

Verse 2

```
Am
   Sun lights up the daytime, moon lights up the night.
                                          E7                       Am
I light up when you call my name, and you know I'm gonna treat you right.

You give me fever when you kiss me, fever when you hold me tight,
                   E7                    Am
Fever in the morning, fever all through the night.

Ev'rybody's got the fever, that is something you all know.
                         E7                  Am
Fever isn't such a new thing, fever started long ago.
```

| **Am** | | **E7** | **Am** |

```
           Am
Verse 3      Romeo loved Juliet, Juliet, she felt the same.
                                                  E7                        Am
           When he put his arms around her, he said, "Julie, baby, you're my flame.

           Thou givest fever when we kisseth, fever with thy flaming youth.
                        E7                  Am
           Fever, I'm afire, fever, yea, I burn for - sooth."
           |Am        |          |E7        |Am        |

           Am
Verse 4    Captain Smith and Pocahontas had a very mad affair.
                                                  E7                       Am
           When her daddy tried to kill him, she said, "Daddy, oh, don't you dare.

           He give me fever with his kisses, fever when he holds me tight.
                                 E7                          Am
           Fever, I'm his missus. Oh, Daddy, won't you treat him right?"

           Am
Verse 5    Now you've listened to my story. Here's the point that I have made.
                                                  E7                  Am
           Chicks were born to give you fever, be it fah - renheit or centi - grade.

           They give you fever when you kiss them, fever if you live you learn.
                           E7                    Am
           Fever, till you sizzle, what a lovely way to burn.
           E7                   Am
           What a lovely way to burn.
           E7                   Am
           What a lovely way to burn.
           E7                   Am    E7  Am
           What a lovely way to burn.
```

Fire on the Mountain

Words by Robert Hunter
Music by Mickey Hart

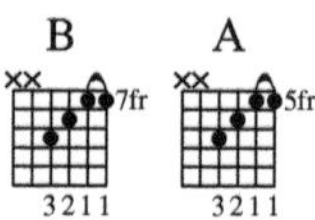

Intro ‖: B | | A | :‖

Verse 1

B Long distance runner, what you (A) standin' there for?
B Get up, get out, (A) get out of the door.
B You're playin' cold music on the (A) barroom floor.
B Drowned in your laughter and (A) dead to the core.
B There's a dragon with matches that's (A) loose on the town.
B Takes a whole pail of water just (A) to cool him down.

Chorus 1

‖: (B) Fire! Fire (A) on the mountain!
(B) Fire! Fire (A) on the mountain! :‖

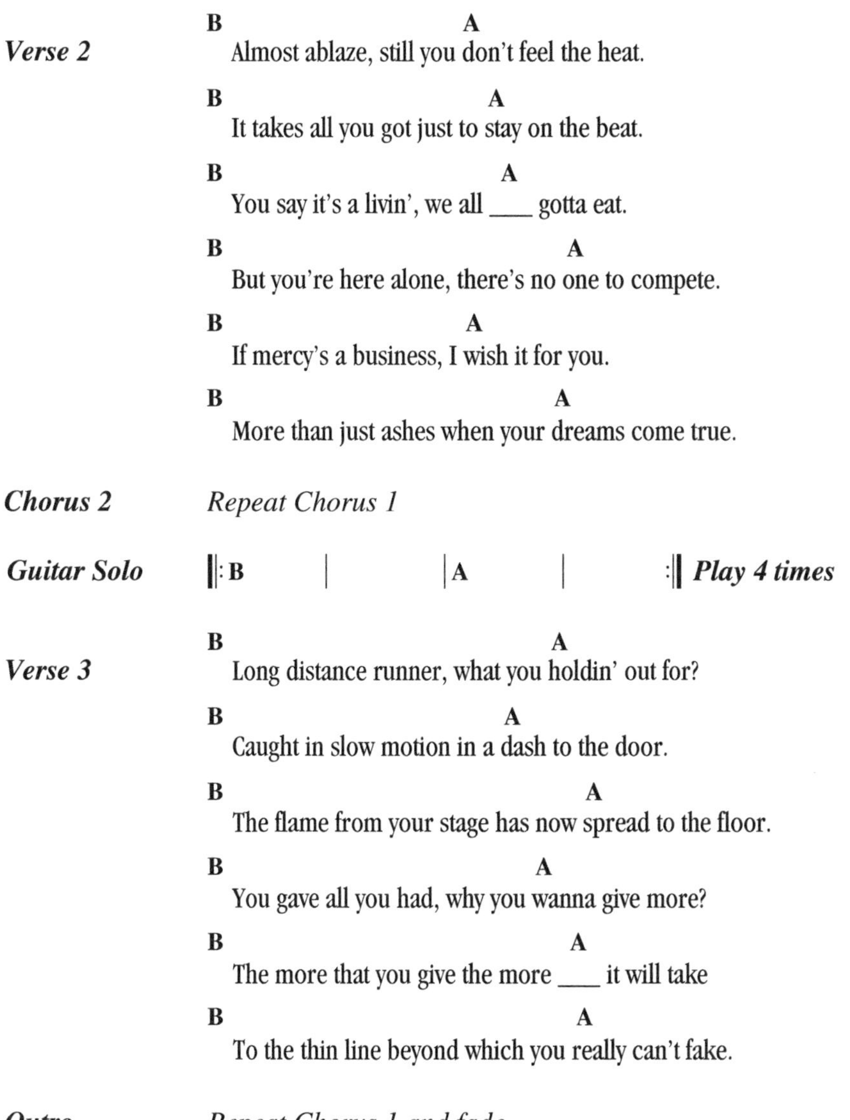

Verse 2

B A
Almost ablaze, still you don't feel the heat.
B A
It takes all you got just to stay on the beat.
B A
You say it's a livin', we all ___ gotta eat.
B A
But you're here alone, there's no one to compete.
B A
If mercy's a business, I wish it for you.
B A
More than just ashes when your dreams come true.

Chorus 2 *Repeat Chorus 1*

Guitar Solo ‖: **B** | | **A** | :‖ ***Play 4 times***

Verse 3

B A
Long distance runner, what you holdin' out for?
B A
Caught in slow motion in a dash to the door.
B A
The flame from your stage has now spread to the floor.
B A
You gave all you had, why you wanna give more?
B A
The more that you give the more ___ it will take
B A
To the thin line beyond which you really can't fake.

Outro *Repeat Chorus 1 and fade*

Get Down Tonight

Words and Music by
Harry Wayne Casey and Richard Finch

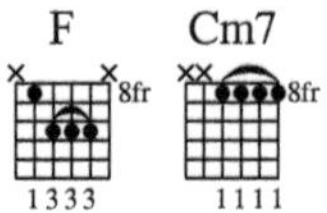

Intro ‖: F | | | :‖

Verse 1

F
Baby, babe, let's get together, honey, honey,

Me and you, and do the things, oh, do the things

That we like to do. Oh!

Chorus 1

Cm7
‖: Do a little dance, make a little love.

F
Get down tonight. Get down tonight. :‖

	F
Verse 2	Baby, babe, I'll meet you someplace, sometime,
	Where we can, oh, get together and ease up our mind. Oh!
Chorus 2	*Repeat Chorus 1*
Keyboard Solo	‖: **F** | | | :‖
Chorus 3	*Repeat Chorus 1*
Interlude	‖: **F** | | | :‖
	F
Outro	‖: Get down, get down, get down, get down, get down tonight, baby.
	Woo, woo, woo, woo, woo, woo, woo, woo, woo, woo.
	Get down, get down, get down, get down, get down tonight, baby.
	No, no, no, no, no, no, no, no, no, no. :‖ ***Repeat and fade***

Heroin

Words and Music by
Lou Reed

Tune down 1/2 step:
(low to high) E♭-A♭-D♭-G♭-B♭-E♭

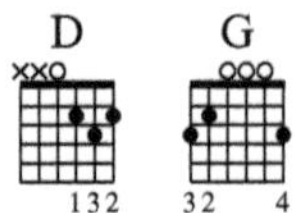


```
Intro      N.C.(D) ||: D      | G      | D      | G      :|| Play 4 times

           D   G            D   G            D       G       D G
Verse 1      I   don't know ___   just where ___ I'm going,

               D      G         D              G          D
           But ___ I'm   gonna try for the kingdom if I can.

                             G                  D
           'Cause it makes me feel like I'm a ___ man

                         G               D
           When I put a spike into my vein.

           Then I tell you things aren't quite the same
                              G             D
           When I'm rush - ing on my run.
                         G              D
           And I feel just like Jesus' son
                             G                  D
           And I guess ___ that I just don't ___ know.
                             G             D
           And I guess ___ that I just don't know.
           | G       | D       | G       | D       | G       |
```

Verse 2

```
D G                D   G    D    G    D G
I ___ have made ___     big deci - sion.
D    G          D G                 D
I'm ___ gonna try     to nullify my ___ life.
                G               D
'Cause when the blood begins to flow,

When it shoots up the dropper's neck,
             G               D
When I'm clos - ing in on death,
           G                 D      G D G
You can't help me, not you ___ guys.
D                G               D
Or all you sweet ___ girls with all your sweet talk.
             G               D
You can all go take a walk.
             G               D
And I guess ___ I just don't know.
             G                   D
And I guess ___ that I just don't ___ know.
| G        | D        | G        | D        | G        |
```

```
            D   G              D  G
Verse 3       I ___ wish that ___    I was born
                               D G D G
            A thousand years ago.
            D    G       D   G                      D
              I ___ wish that    I'd sailed the darkened ___ seas
                      G              D
            On a great ___ big clipper ship
                         G               D
            Going from this ___ land here to that,
                        G               D G D G
            Ah, it's in a sail - or's suit and cap,

            Away from the big city,
            D              G             D
            Where a man ___ cannot be free
                      G           D
            Of all the e - vils of this town
                        G               D
            And of him - self and those a - round.
                         G             D
            Oh, and I guess ___ that I just don't know.
                         G                    D
            Oh, and I guess ___ that I just don't know.
                 G                 D        G D G
            Her - oin, be the death ___ of me.

            Heroin, it's my wife and it's my life.

            D        G           D G             D G D G
Verse 4     Because ___ a main   -   er to my vein
            D    G       D      G          D
            Beats to a cen - ter in my head,
                           G       D          G D G D
            And then I'm bet - ter off than dead.
            | G        | D        | G        | D        | G        |
```

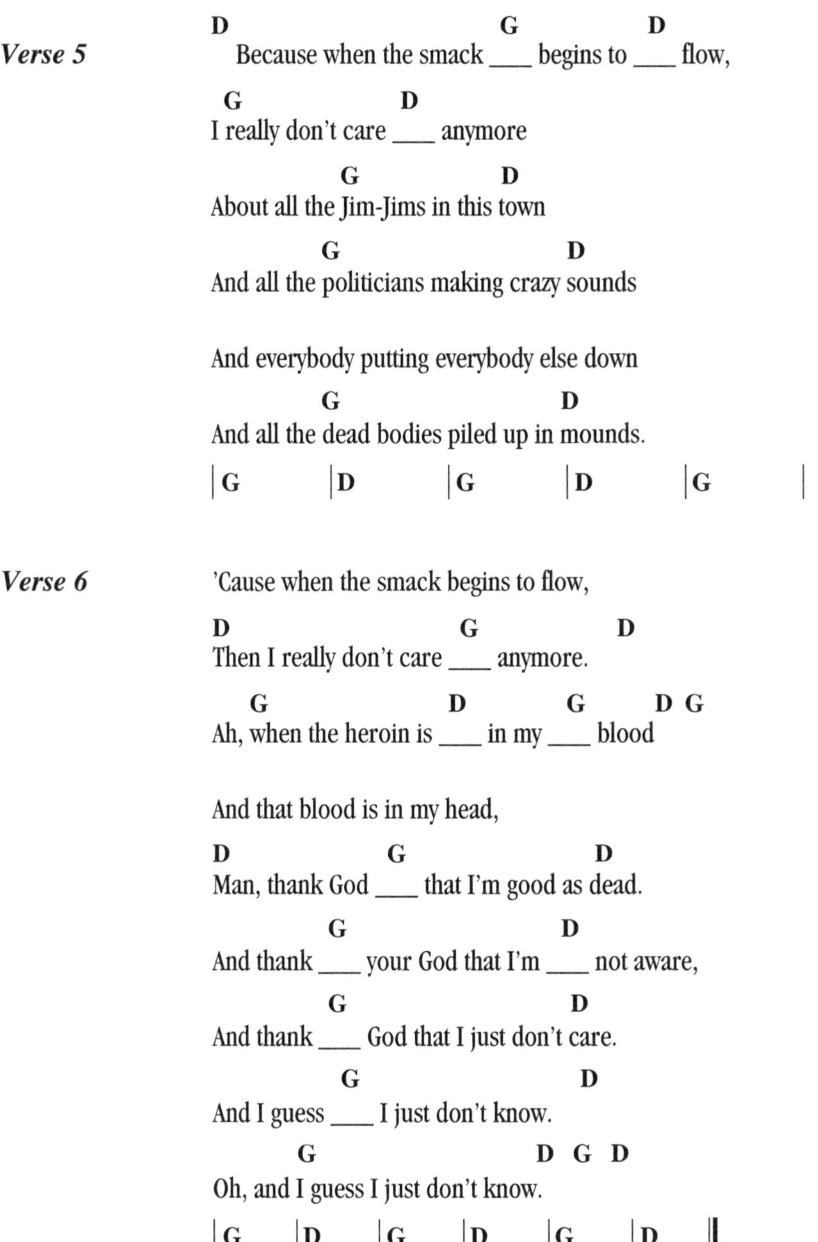

Verse 5

D G D
Because when the smack ___ begins to ___ flow,

G D
I really don't care ___ anymore

G D
About all the Jim-Jims in this town

G D
And all the politicians making crazy sounds

And everybody putting everybody else down

G D
And all the dead bodies piled up in mounds.

| G | D | G | D | G |

Verse 6

'Cause when the smack begins to flow,

D G D
Then I really don't care ___ anymore.

G D G D G
Ah, when the heroin is ___ in my ___ blood

And that blood is in my head,

D G D
Man, thank God ___ that I'm good as dead.

G D
And thank ___ your God that I'm ___ not aware,

G D
And thank ___ God that I just don't care.

G D
And I guess ___ I just don't know.

G D G D
Oh, and I guess I just don't know.

| G | D | G | D | G | D ||

Hey Gyp
(Dig the Slowness)

Words and Music by
Donovan Leitch

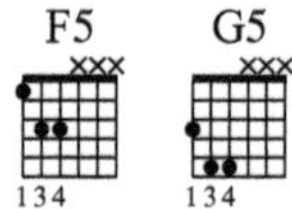


```
Intro      F5  |G5  F5  |G5  F5  |G5  F5  |G5  F5  |G5  F5  |

              G5                    F5   G5                   F5
Verse 1    I'll buy you a Chevrolet, ___ buy you a Chevrolet,

              G5          F5
           I'll buy you a Chevrolet.

           G5                         F5   G5                             F5
           Just give me some of your love, just give me some of your love,

           G5                         F5        G5                             F5
           Just give me some of your love, gal, just give me some of your love.

                  G5                      F5        G5                     F5
Verse 2    I don't want your Chevrolet, ___ I don't want your Chevrolet,

                  G5          F5
           I don't want your Chevrolet.

           G5                         F5        G5                             F5
           Just give me some of your love, man, just give me some of your love.

                   G5                          F5        G5                             F5
           If you just give me some of your love, man, just give me some of your love.
```

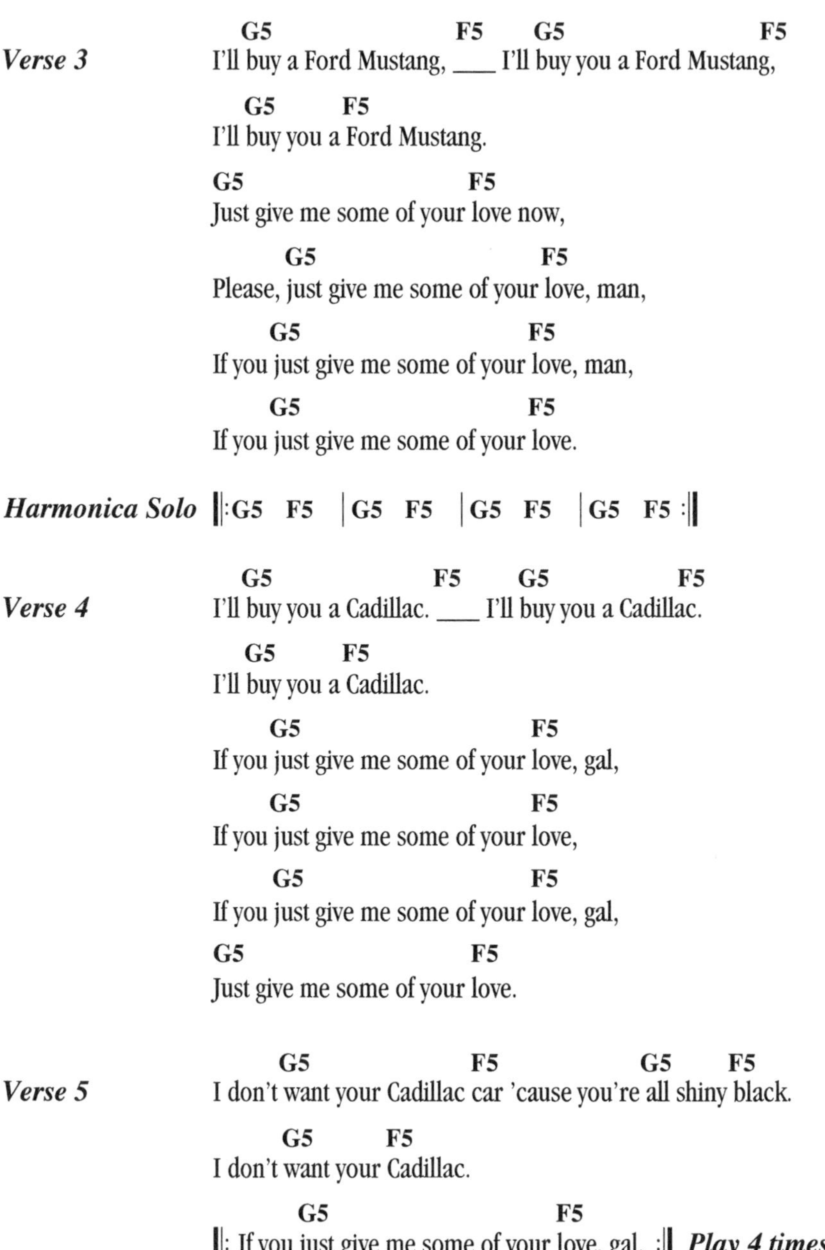

Verse 3

G5 F5 G5 F5
I'll buy a Ford Mustang, ___ I'll buy you a Ford Mustang,

G5 F5
I'll buy you a Ford Mustang.

G5 F5
Just give me some of your love now,

G5 F5
Please, just give me some of your love, man,

G5 F5
If you just give me some of your love, man,

G5 F5
If you just give me some of your love.

Harmonica Solo **‖: G5 F5 | G5 F5 | G5 F5 | G5 F5 :‖**

Verse 4

G5 F5 G5 F5
I'll buy you a Cadillac. ___ I'll buy you a Cadillac.

G5 F5
I'll buy you a Cadillac.

G5 F5
If you just give me some of your love, gal,

G5 F5
If you just give me some of your love,

G5 F5
If you just give me some of your love, gal,

G5 F5
Just give me some of your love.

Verse 5

G5 F5 G5 F5
I don't want your Cadillac car 'cause you're all shiny black.

G5 F5
I don't want your Cadillac.

G5 F5
‖: If you just give me some of your love, gal. :‖ ***Play 4 times***

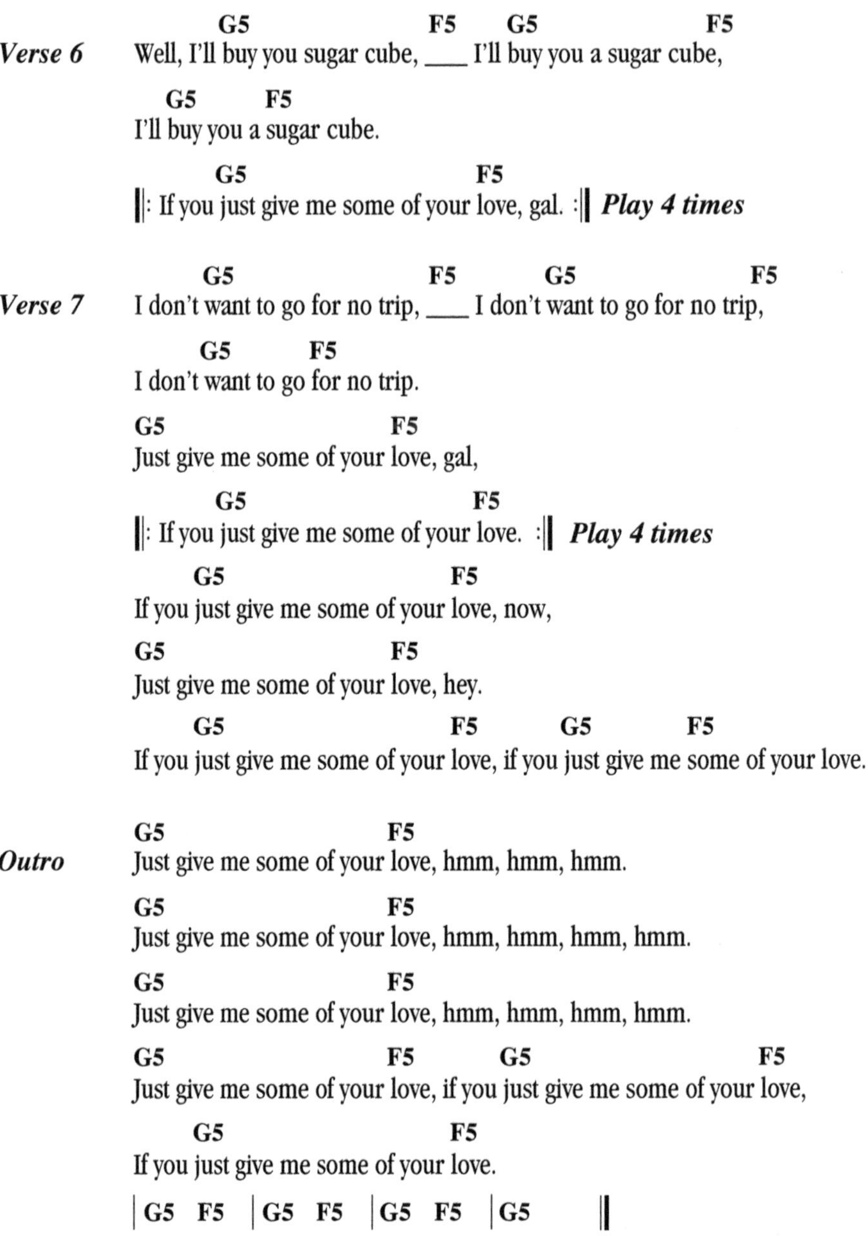

Verse 6

G5 F5 G5 F5
Well, I'll buy you sugar cube, ___ I'll buy you a sugar cube,

G5 F5
I'll buy you a sugar cube.

G5 F5
‖: If you just give me some of your love, gal. :‖ ***Play 4 times***

Verse 7

G5 F5 G5 F5
I don't want to go for no trip, ___ I don't want to go for no trip,

G5 F5
I don't want to go for no trip.

G5 F5
Just give me some of your love, gal,

G5 F5
‖: If you just give me some of your love. :‖ ***Play 4 times***

G5 F5
If you just give me some of your love, now,

G5 F5
Just give me some of your love, hey.

G5 F5 G5 F5
If you just give me some of your love, if you just give me some of your love.

Outro

G5 F5
Just give me some of your love, hmm, hmm, hmm.

G5 F5
Just give me some of your love, hmm, hmm, hmm, hmm.

G5 F5
Just give me some of your love, hmm, hmm, hmm, hmm.

G5 F5 G5 F5
Just give me some of your love, if you just give me some of your love,

G5 F5
If you just give me some of your love.

| G5 F5 | G5 F5 | G5 F5 | G5 ‖

A Horse with No Name

Words and Music by
Dewey Bunnell

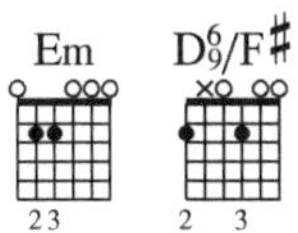

Intro ‖: Em | D6/9/F# :‖

Verse 1

Em D6/9/F#
On the first part of the jour - ney

Em D6/9/F#
I was looking at all the life.

Em D6/9/F#
There were plants and birds and rocks ___ and things,

Em D6/9/F#
There were sand and hills and rings.

Em D6/9/F#
The first thing I met was a fly with a buzz

Em D6/9/F#
And the sky with no clouds.

Em D6/9/F#
The heat was hot and the ground was dry,

Em D6/9/F#
But the air was full of sound.

Chorus 1

```
      Em                          D6/9/F#
I've been thru the desert on a horse with no name.

       Em                      D6/9/F#
It felt good to be out of the rain.

        Em                  D6/9/F#
In the desert you can re - member your name

               Em                  D6/9/F#
'Cause there ain't no one for to give you no pain.
```

Interlude 1

```
   Em       D6/9/F#                       Em   D6/9/F#
||: La, la, la, ____ la, la, la, la, la, la, la, la, la.  :||
```

Verse 2

```
       Em              D6/9/F#
After two days in the desert sun

    Em                 D6/9/F#
My skin began to turn red.

       Em              D6/9/F#
After three days in the desert fun

       Em                  D6/9/F#
I was looking at a river bed.

           Em             D6/9/F#
And the story it told of a river that flowed

              Em                D6/9/F#
Made me sad to think it was dead.
```

Chorus 2

```
                Em                          D6/9/F#
You see I've been thru the desert on a horse with no name.

       Em                      D6/9/F#
It felt good to be out of the rain.

        Em                  D6/9/F#
In the desert you can re - member your name

               Em                  D6/9/F#
'Cause there ain't no one for to give you no pain.
```

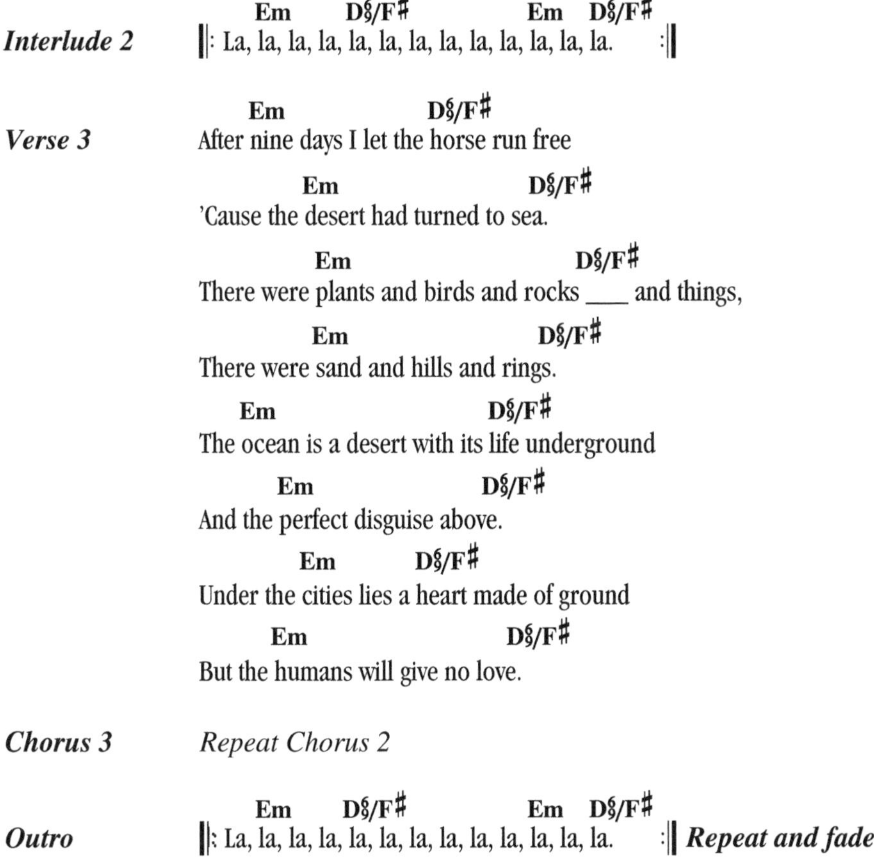

Interlude 2

Em D6/9/F# Em D6/9/F#
‖: La, la, la, la, la, la, la, la, la, la, la, la, la. :‖

Verse 3

Em D6/9/F#
After nine days I let the horse run free

Em D6/9/F#
'Cause the desert had turned to sea.

Em D6/9/F#
There were plants and birds and rocks ___ and things,

Em D6/9/F#
There were sand and hills and rings.

Em D6/9/F#
The ocean is a desert with its life underground

Em D6/9/F#
And the perfect disguise above.

Em D6/9/F#
Under the cities lies a heart made of ground

Em D6/9/F#
But the humans will give no love.

Chorus 3

Repeat Chorus 2

Outro

Em D6/9/F# Em D6/9/F#
‖: La, la, la, la, la, la, la, la, la, la, la, la, la. :‖ ***Repeat and fade***

Hey Liley, Liley Lo
(Married Man Gonna Keep Your Secret)

Words and Music by Elizabeth Austin and Alan Lomax
Additional Words and Music by Alan Lomax

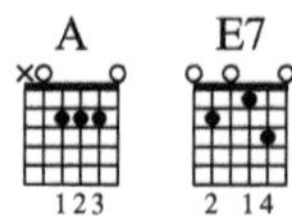

Chorus 1

```
   A
‖: Hey liley, liley-ley,
              E7
Hey liley, liley lo.

Hey liley, liley-ley,
              A
Hey liley, liley lo. :‖
```

Verse 1

```
   A                                  E7
In college once I learned a phrase, (Hey liley, liley lo.)
                                   A
It saved my life on many days. (Hey liley, liley lo.)
                                          E7
These words have meaning just for me. (Hey liley, liley lo.)
                                   A
They followed my philosophy. (Hey liley, liley lo.)
```

Chorus 2

```
A
Hey liley, liley-ley,
          E7
Hey liley, liley lo.

Hey liley, liley-ley,
          A
Hey liley, liley lo. The message.
```

Verse 2

```
   A                                E7
I've never faced a problem yet (Hey liley, liley lo.)
                                            A
That's ever caused me any sweat. (Hey liley, liley lo.)
                                  E7
My income tax is overdue. (Hey liley, liley lo.)
                                                A
The local draft board wants me too. (Hey liley, liley lo.)
```

Chorus 3

```
A
Hey liley, liley-ley,
          E7
Hey liley, liley lo.

Hey liley, liley-ley,
          A
Hey liley, liley lo. What else?
```

Verse 3

```
    A                                 E7
Now life for me is just a breeze. (Hey liley, liley lo.)
                               A
I give advice to Ph.Ds. (Hey liley, liley lo.)
                                                      E7
There's just one question left for man (Hey liley, liley lo.)
N.C.                                  E7        A
Whose idea was the Edsel anyway? (Hey liley, liley lo.)
```

Chorus 4 — *Repeat Chorus 1*

The Hokey Pokey

Words and Music by Charles P. Macak,
Tafft Baker and Larry LaPrise

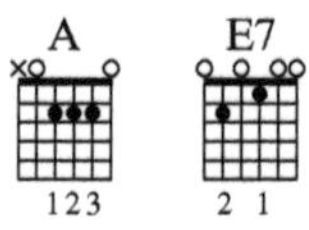

Verse 1

A
You put your right foot in,

You put your right foot out,

You put your right foot in,

E7
And you shake it all about.

Chorus 1

You do the Hokey Pokey

And you turn yourself around.

A
That's what it's all a-bout.

You do the Hokey Pokey.

E7
You do the Hokey Pokey.

You do the Hokey Pokey.

A
That's what it's all a-bout.

	A
Verse 2	You put your left foot in,
	You put your left foot out,
	You put your left foot in,
	E7
	And you shake it all about.
Chorus 2	***Repeat Chorus 1***
	A
Verse 3	You put your right arm in,
	You put your right arm out,
	You put your right arm in,
	E7
	And you shake it all about.
Chorus 3	***Repeat Chorus 1***
	A
Verse 4	You put your left arm in,
	You put your left arm out,
	You put your left arm in,
	E7
	And you shake it all about.
Chorus 4	***Repeat Chorus 1***

	A
Verse 5	You put your right elbow in,
	You put your right elbow out,
	You put your right elbow in,
	E7
	And you shake it all about.
Chorus 5	***Repeat Chorus 1***
	A
Verse 6	You put your left elbow in,
	You put your left elbow out,
	You put your left elbow in,
	E7
	And you shake it all about.
Chorus 6	***Repeat Chorus 1***
	A
Verse 7	You put your head in,
	You put your head out,
	You put your head in,
	E7
	And you shake it all about.
Chorus 7	***Repeat Chorus 1***

	A
Verse 8	You put your right hip in,
	You put your right hip out,
	You put your right hip in,
	E7
	And you shake it all about.

Chorus 8 ***Repeat Chorus 1***

	A
Verse 9	You put your left hip in,
	You put your left hip out,
	You put your left hip in,
	E7
	And you shake it all about.

Chorus 9 ***Repeat Chorus 1***

	A
Verse 10	You put your whole self in,
	You put your whole self out,
	You put your whole self in,
	E7
	And you shake it all about.

Chorus 10 ***Repeat Chorus 1***

Honky Tonkin'

Words and Music by
Hank Williams

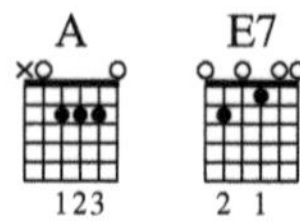

Verse 1

```
         A
When you are sad and lonely

And have no place to go,

Just come to see me, baby,

And bring along some dough.

And we'll go honky tonkin', honky tonkin',

Honky tonkin', honey baby.
                        E7        A
We'll go honky tonkin' 'round this town.
```

Verse 2

```
         A
When you and your baby
Have a fallin' out
Just call me up, sweet mama,
And we'll go steppin' out.
And we'll go honky tonkin', honky tonkin',
Honky tonkin', honey baby.
                            E7        A
We'll go honky tonkin' 'round this town.
```

Verse 3

```
         A
We're goin' to the city,
To the city fair.
If you go to the city
Then you will find me there.
And we'll go honky tonkin', honky tonkin',
Honky tonkin', honey baby.
                            E7        A
We'll go honky tonkin' 'round this town.
```

Verse 4 ***Repeat Verse 1***

I Love You a Thousand Ways

Words and Music by
Lefty Frizzell and James A. Beck

Melody:

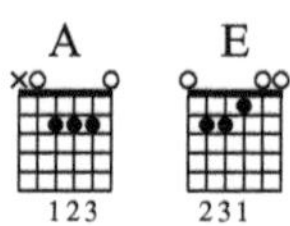

Intro | A | | E | |

Verse 1

```
     A                        E
I love you, I'll prove it in days to come.
                                       A
I swear it's true, darling, you're the only one.
                                   E
I think of you, of the past and all our fun.
                              A
I love you, I'll prove it in days to come.
          E
You're my darling, you've been true.
       A
I should have been good to you.
          E                              A
You're the one that's in my heart while we're a - part.
```

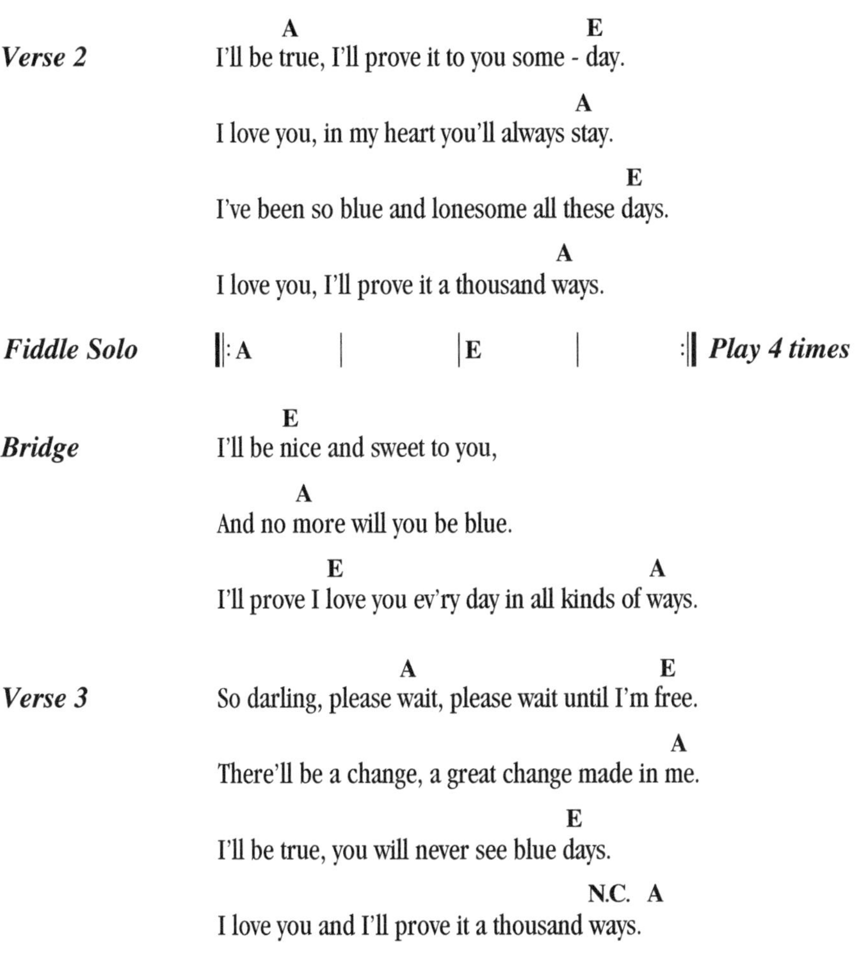

Verse 2

A E
I'll be true, I'll prove it to you some - day.

A
I love you, in my heart you'll always stay.

E
I've been so blue and lonesome all these days.

A
I love you, I'll prove it a thousand ways.

Fiddle Solo ‖: A | | E | :‖ *Play 4 times*

Bridge

E
I'll be nice and sweet to you,

A
And no more will you be blue.

E A
I'll prove I love you ev'ry day in all kinds of ways.

Verse 3

A E
So darling, please wait, please wait until I'm free.

A
There'll be a change, a great change made in me.

E
I'll be true, you will never see blue days.

N.C. A
I love you and I'll prove it a thousand ways.

I Need to Know

Words and Music by
Cory Rooney and Marc Anthony

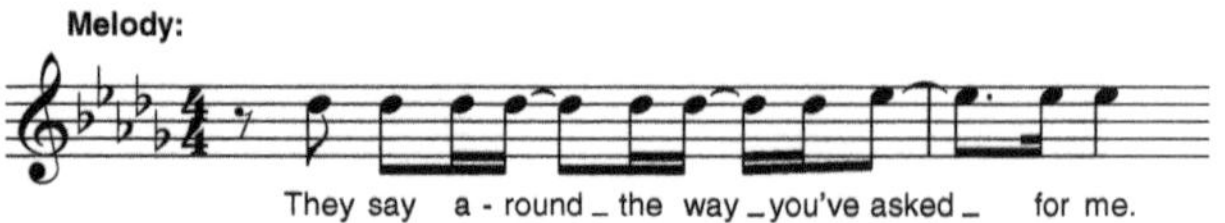

(Capo 1st fret)

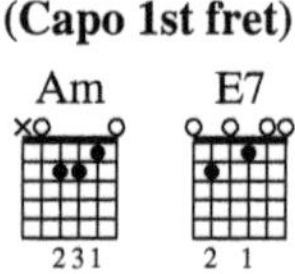

Intro ‖: Am | E7 | | Am :‖ *Play 4 times*

Verse 1

Am **E7**
They say around the way you've asked ___ for me.

Am
There's even talk about you wanting me.

E7
I must admit that's what I want to hear,

Am
But that's just talk until you take me there.

Chorus 1

```
        Am                                    E7
Oh, if ___ it's true don't leave me all a - lone out here,
                                           Am
Wond'ring this if you're ever gonna take me there.
                                           E7
Tell me what you're feeling 'cause I need to know.
                                              Am
Girl, you've got to let me know which way to go
                                     E7
'Cause I need to know. I need to know.
                                Am
Tell me, baby, girl, 'cause I need to know.
                         E7
I need to know. I need to know.
                                Am
Tell me, baby, girl, 'cause I need to know.
```

Verse 2

```
Am                                 E7
     My ev'ry thought is of this be - ing true.
                             Am
It's getting harder not to think of you.
                          E7
Girl, I'm exactly where I wanna be.
                                 Am
The only thing's I need you here with me.
```

Chorus 2

Repeat Chorus 1

Interlude | Am | E7 | | Am |

Chorus 3

```
                    Am              E7
||: 'Cause I need to know. I need to know.
                              Am
Tell me, baby, girl, 'cause I need to know.
                        E7
I need to know. I need to know.
                              Am
Tell me, baby, girl, 'cause I need to know.
                                  E7
If it's true don't leave me all a - lone out here,
                                    Am
Wond'ring if you're ever gonna take me there.
                                        E7
Tell me what you're feeling 'cause I need to know.
                                          Am
Girl, you've gotta let me know which way to go. :||
              N.C.
'Cause I need to know. I need to know.

Tell me, baby, girl, 'cause I need to know.

I need to know. I need to know.

Tell me, baby, girl, 'cause I need to know.
```

Iko Iko

Words and Music by Rosa Lee Hawkins, Barbara Ann Hawkins, Joan Marie Johnson, Joe Jones, Maralyn Jones, Sharon Jones and Jessie Thomas

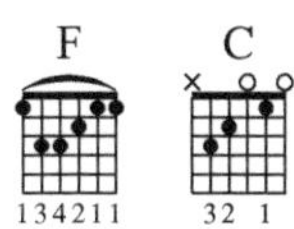

Intro ‖: N.C. (Cowbell) :‖ ***Play 6 times***

Verse 1

N.C.
My Grandma and your Grandma were sitting by the fire.

My Grandma says to your Grandma, "I'm gonna set your flag on fire."

Chorus 1

N.C.
Talkin' 'bout hey now! Hey now! Iko, Iko, unday.

Jockamo feeno ai nane. Jockamo fee nane.

Verse 2

F C
Look at my king all dressed in red. Iko, Iko, un - day.

I betcha five dollars he'll kill you dead.

F
Jockamo fee na - ne.

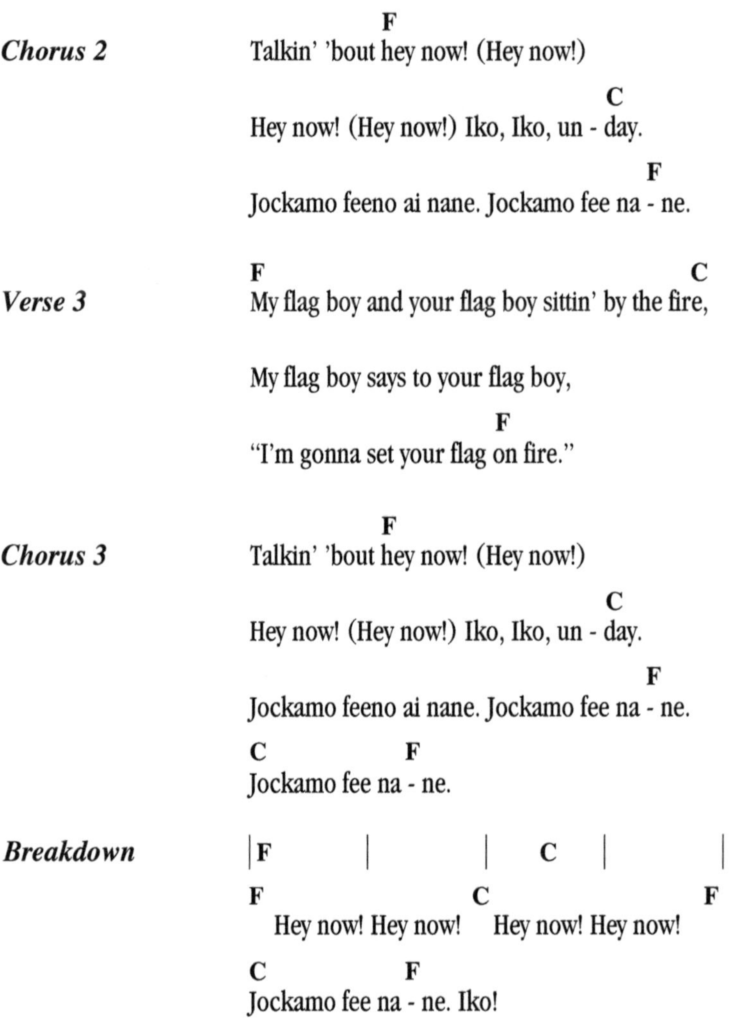

Chorus 2

F
Talkin' 'bout hey now! (Hey now!)

C
Hey now! (Hey now!) Iko, Iko, un - day.

F
Jockamo feeno ai nane. Jockamo fee na - ne.

Verse 3

F C
My flag boy and your flag boy sittin' by the fire,

My flag boy says to your flag boy,

F
"I'm gonna set your flag on fire."

Chorus 3

F
Talkin' 'bout hey now! (Hey now!)

C
Hey now! (Hey now!) Iko, Iko, un - day.

F
Jockamo feeno ai nane. Jockamo fee na - ne.

C F
Jockamo fee na - ne.

Breakdown

| F | | C | |

F C F
Hey now! Hey now! Hey now! Hey now!

C F
Jockamo fee na - ne. Iko!

Verse 4

F
See that man all dressed in green?

C
Iko, Iko, un - day.

He's not a man, he's a lovin' machine.

F
Jockamo fee na - ne.

Chorus 4

F
‖: Talkin' 'bout hey now! (Hey now!)

C
Hey now! (Hey now!) Iko, Iko, un - day.

F
Jockamo feeno ai nane. Jockamo fee na - ne. :‖

Outro

C F
‖: Jockamo fee na - ne. :‖ ***Repeat and fade***

I Want Candy

Words and Music by
Bert Berns, Bob Feldman,
Jerry Goldstein and Richard Gottehrer

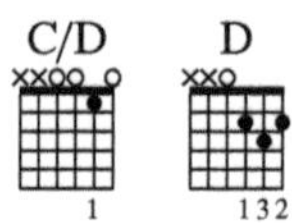

Intro ||: N.C. | | | :||
| C/D D | N.C. C/D D | N.C. C/D D | N.C. C/D D |

Verse 1

N.C. C/D D
I know a guy who's tough but sweet.

N.C. C/D D
He so fine, he can't be beat.

N.C. C/D D
He's got ev'rything I desire.

C/D D
Sets the summer sun on fire.

Chorus 1

D C/D D C/D D
I want Can - dy,

C/D D C/D D
I want Can - dy.

Interlude 1 | N.C. | | C/D D | N.C. C/D D |

Verse 2

```
N.C.                                    C/D D
Go to see him when the sun goes down.

N.C.                       C/D D
Ain't no finer boy in town.

N.C.                                          C/D D
You're my guy, just what the doctor ordered.

N.C.                                 C/D D
So sweet you make my mouth water.
```

Chorus 2 — *Repeat Chorus 1*

Interlude 2

```
‖: N.C.(D)    :‖
```

Play 10 times

Verse 3

```
N.C.(D)
Candy on the beach, there's nothing better.

But I like Candy when it's wrapped in a sweater.

Someday soon, I'll make you mine.

                            C/D D
And I'll have Candy all the time.
```

Chorus 3

```
   D          C/D D C/D D
‖: I want Can  -  dy,

          C/D D C/D D
I want Can  -  dy.        :‖

N.C.
```

Hey! Hey! Hey! Hey! Hey!

I'd Rather Go Blind

Words and Music by
Ellington Jordan and Billy Foster

Melody:
Some-thing told me it was o - ver

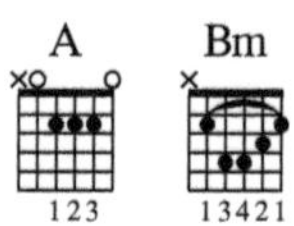
A
123
Bm
13421

Intro | A | Bm | | A |

Verse 1

A **Bm**
Something told me it was over

A
When I saw you and her talking.

Bm
Something down deep in my soul said, "Cry girl,"

A
When I saw you and that girl walking.

Chorus 1

A **Bm**
I would rather, I would rather go blind, boy,

A
Than to see you walk away from me.

Verse 2

```
A                              Bm
   So you see, I love you so much,

And I don't wanna watch you leave me, baby.

                              A
But most of all, I just don't wanna be free.

                 Bm
I was just, I was just, I was just sitting here thinking

                               A
Of your kiss and your warm embrace,

                                          Bm
When the reflection in the glass that I held to my lips, baby,

                                     A
Revealed the tears that was on my face.
```

Outro-Chorus

```
    A                 Bm
||:   I would rather be blind, boy,

Than to see you walk away from me. :||
```
Repeat and fade

It's Your Thing

Words and Music by Rudolph Isley, Ronald Isley and O'Kelly Isley

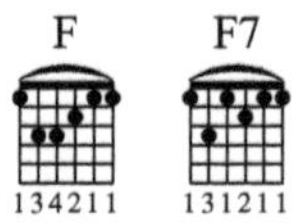

Intro ‖: N.C.(F) | :‖

Chorus 1

```
          N.C.(F)
It's your thing, do what you wanna do.

I can't tell ya who to sock it to.

It's your thing, do what you wanna do, yeah.

I can't tell you ya who to sock it to.
```

Verse 1

```
                 F7
If ya want me to love ya, maybe I will, ha.

If I need me a woman, it ain't no big deal.

Ah, you need love now just the same as I do.

Makes me no diff'rence now who ya give your thing to.
```

Chorus 2

N.C.(F)
Oh, it's your thing, do what you wanna do.

I can't tell ya who to sock it to.

It's your thing, do what you wanna do, now.

I can't tell you ya who to sock it to.

Interlude

F7
Oh, ___ yeah. Alright. *Lord, have mercy.*

Chorus 3

Repeat Chorus 1

Verse 2

F7
I'm not tryin' to run your life.

I know you wanna do what's right.

Oh, give your love, girl, to whoever you choose.

How can you lose with the stuff you use, now?

Chorus 4

N.C.(F)
It's your thing, do what you wanna do.

I can't tell ya who to sock it to.

It's your thing, do what you wanna do.

Don't let me tell ya who to sock it to.

Let me know ya say it's my thing.

I do what I wanna do.

I can't tell ya who to sock it to. ***Fade out***

Jambalaya (On the Bayou)

Words and Music by
Hank Williams

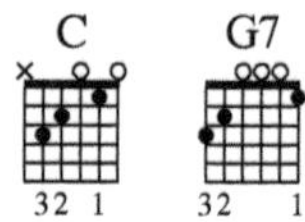


```
                 C                   G7
Verse 1          Goodbye Joe, me gotta go, me oh my oh.
                                                C
                 Me gotta go pole the pirogue down the bayou.
                                                G7
                 My Yvonne, the sweetest one, me oh my oh.
                                                C
                 Son of a gun, we'll have big fun on the bayou.

                 C                           G7
Chorus 1         Jamba-laya and crawfish pie and filé gumbo
                                                     C
                 'Cause tonight I'm a gonna see my ma cher a-mio.
                                           G7
                 Pick guitar, fill fruit jar, and be gay-o.
                                                C
                 Son of a gun, we'll have big fun on the bayou.
```

Verse 2

```
    C                                      G7
Thibo-daux, Fontaineaux, the place is buzzin',
                                      C
Kinfolk come to see Yvonne by the dozen.
                                           G7
Dress in style and go hog wild, me oh my oh.
                                           C
Son of a gun, we'll have big fun on the bayou.
```

Chorus 2 ***Repeat Chorus 1***

Verse 3

```
     C                                      G7
Settle down far from town, get me a pi-rogue,
                                   C
And I'll catch all the fish in the bayou.
                                             G7
Swap my mon to buy Yvonne what she need o,
                                             C
Son of a gun, we'll have big fun on the bayou.
```

Chorus 3 ***Repeat Chorus 1***

Jane Says

Words and Music by Perry Farrell, Dave Navarro, Stephen Perkins and Eric Avery

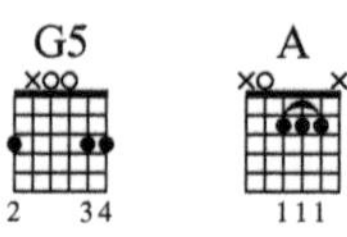

Intro ‖: G5 A | G5 A :‖

Verse 1

```
G5         A        G5              A
Jane says, ___ "I'm done with Sergi - o;
G5 A                          G5      A
     He treat me like a rag ___ doll."
G5          A       G5       A
She hides ___ her television.
G5 A                          G5    A
     Says, "I don't owe him noth - ing.
G5   A                        G5            A
But if he comes back again,     tell him to wait right here for me
G5   A              G5        A
   Or try again tomor - row."
```

Chorus 1

```
G5
   "I'm gon - na kick tomor  -  row.

   I'm gon - na kick to - mor - row."
```

Interlude 1 *Repeat Intro*

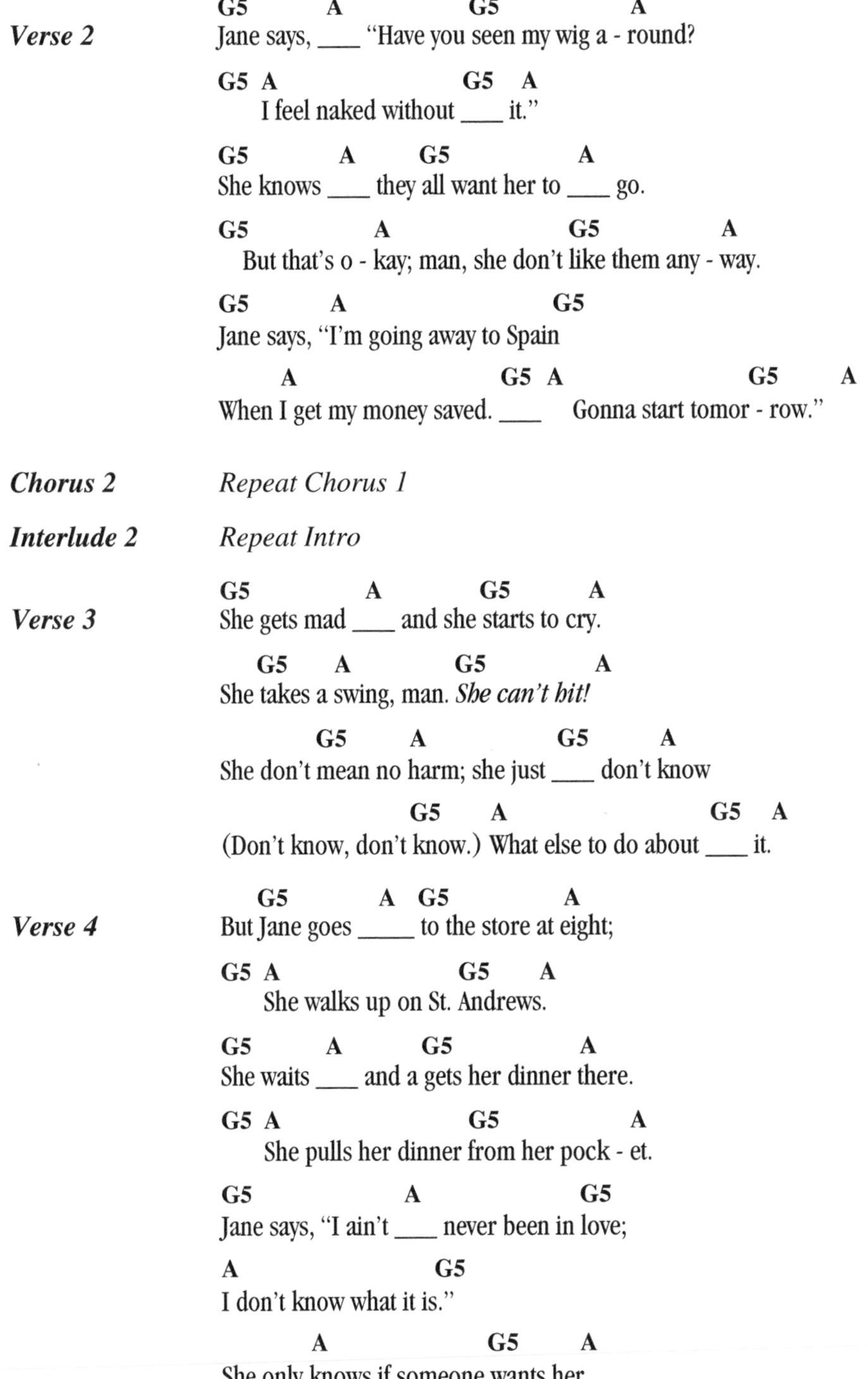

Verse 2

G5 A G5 A
Jane says, ___ "Have you seen my wig a - round?

G5 A G5 A
I feel naked without ___ it."

G5 A G5 A
She knows ___ they all want her to ___ go.

G5 A G5 A
But that's o - kay; man, she don't like them any - way.

G5 A G5
Jane says, "I'm going away to Spain

A G5 A G5 A
When I get my money saved. ___ Gonna start tomor - row."

Chorus 2 *Repeat Chorus 1*

Interlude 2 *Repeat Intro*

Verse 3

G5 A G5 A
She gets mad ___ and she starts to cry.

G5 A G5 A
She takes a swing, man. *She can't hit!*

G5 A G5 A
She don't mean no harm; she just ___ don't know

G5 A G5 A
(Don't know, don't know.) What else to do about ___ it.

Verse 4

G5 A G5 A
But Jane goes ____ to the store at eight;

G5 A G5 A
She walks up on St. Andrews.

G5 A G5 A
She waits ___ and a gets her dinner there.

G5 A G5 A
She pulls her dinner from her pock - et.

G5 A G5
Jane says, "I ain't ___ never been in love;

A G5
I don't know what it is."

A G5 A
She only knows if someone wants her.

```
Chorus 3       G5
                 "I want 'em if they want me.

                 I only know they want me."

Interlude 3    Repeat Intro

               G5              A            G5          A
Verse 5        She gets mad ___ and she starts to cry.

                   G5     A             G5            A
               She takes a swing, man. She can't hit!

                          G5        A                 G5        A
               She don't mean no harm; she just ___ don't know

                                    G5      A                         G5    A
               (Don't know, don't know.) What else to do about ___ it.
               G5
               Jane ___ says...

               Jane ______ says...

Outro          | G5    A       | G5      A              |
                 Ah. ____________________ Hoo, hoo, hoo,

               | G5    A       | G5      A              |
                         Hoo, hoo, hoo, hoo.

               ||: G5       A      :|| Play 5 times
               ||: G5              :|| Play 4 times
               ||: G5       A      :|| Repeat and fade
```

Looking at You

Words and Music by Fred Smith,
Michael Davis, Dennis Thompson,
Wayne Kramer and Robert Derminer

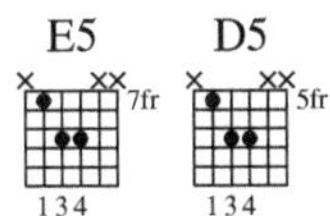

Intro ‖: E5 | D5 :‖

Verse 1

```
E5             D5       E5                      D5
   When it hap - pened     something snapped ___ inside,
      E5                  D5         E5                D5
Made me want to hide ___ all a - lone on my own,
      E5              D5
All a - lone on my own.
E5                  D5                        E5                 D5
   I stood up on ___ the stand with my ___ eyes shut tight.
                     E5            D5
Didn't want to see ___ anybody     feeling happy,
E5                         D5
Havin' a good time, now, hey,
          E5                  D5
Doin' al - right, doin' alright,
          E5                  D5
Doin' al - right, doin' alright.
```

```
Guitar Solo 1    ||: E5          | D5          :|| Play 10 times

                 E5                  D5                     E5
Verse 2             Line stalled into ___ the dancing crowd,

                            D5
                 Felt like screaming out loud.

                 E5           D5
                    I saw you standing there,

                   E5              D5                    E5  D5
                 I saw your long,     saw your long hair.

                 E5             D5             E5                D5
                    Open up my     eyes, baby,     you made me      realize

                      E5               D5      E5                D5
                 All I want to do now,     all I want to do now, girl...

                                 E5                        D5
Chorus 1         Is look at you, ___ looking at you, baby,

                               E5                        D5
                 Look at you, ___ looking at you, baby,

                             E5  D5
                 Yeah, yeah, hey.

Guitar Solo 2    Repeat Guitar Solo 1
```

Verse 3

```
E5                  D5              E5
   Line stalled into ___ the dancing crowd,
          D5
I felt like    screaming out loud.
E5                D5
   All I wanna do,    all I wanna do,
E5               D5
   All I want to do...
```

Chorus 2

```
               E5                      D5
Is look at you, ___ looking at you, baby,
             E5                      D5
Look at you, ___ looking at you, baby,
                E5   D5            E5     D5
Looking at you, ___     looking at ___ you,
            E5              D5        E5
Looking at ___ you, baby,    you baby,
          D5          E5 D5 E5 D5
You baby,    you baby, yeah.
```

Outro-Guitar Solo *Repeat Guitar Solo 1 and fade*

Lady In Black

Words and Music by
Ken Hensley

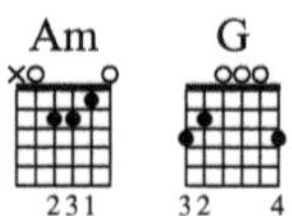

Intro | Am | |

Verse 1

Am
She came to me one mornin', one lonely Sunday morning,

G   Am
Her long hair flowing in the mid-winter wind.

I know not how she found me, for in darkness I was walking,

G   Am
And de - struction lay around me from a fight ___ I could not win.

Am   G   Am   G   Am
Ah, ah, ah, ah, ah, ah, ah, ah, ah. Ah, ah, ah, ah, ah, ah, ah.

Verse 2

Am
She asked me name my foe then I said the need within some men

G   Am
To fight and kill their brothers without thought of love or God.

And I begged her give me horses to trample down my enemies,

G   Am
So eager was my passion to de - vour this waste of life.

Am   G   Am   G   Am
Ah, ah, ah, ah, ah, ah, ah, ah, ah. Ah, ah, ah, ah, ah, ah, ah.

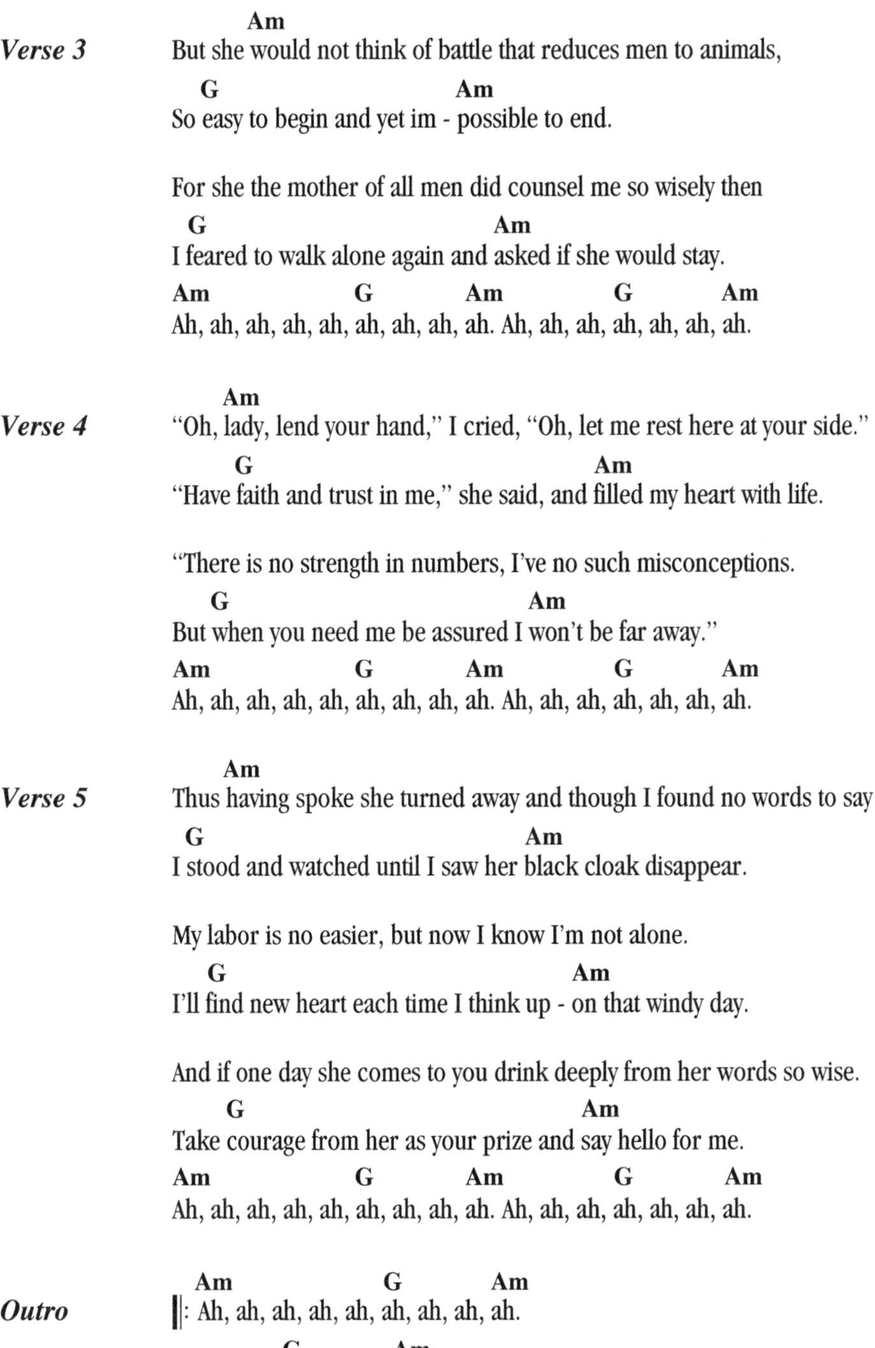

Verse 3

Am
But she would not think of battle that reduces men to animals,
G **Am**
So easy to begin and yet im - possible to end.

For she the mother of all men did counsel me so wisely then
G **Am**
I feared to walk alone again and asked if she would stay.
Am **G** **Am** **G** **Am**
Ah, ah, ah, ah, ah, ah, ah, ah, ah. Ah, ah, ah, ah, ah, ah, ah.

Verse 4

Am
"Oh, lady, lend your hand," I cried, "Oh, let me rest here at your side."
G **Am**
"Have faith and trust in me," she said, and filled my heart with life.

"There is no strength in numbers, I've no such misconceptions.
G **Am**
But when you need me be assured I won't be far away."
Am **G** **Am** **G** **Am**
Ah, ah, ah, ah, ah, ah, ah, ah, ah. Ah, ah, ah, ah, ah, ah, ah.

Verse 5

Am
Thus having spoke she turned away and though I found no words to say
G **Am**
I stood and watched until I saw her black cloak disappear.

My labor is no easier, but now I know I'm not alone.
G **Am**
I'll find new heart each time I think up - on that windy day.

And if one day she comes to you drink deeply from her words so wise.
G **Am**
Take courage from her as your prize and say hello for me.
Am **G** **Am** **G** **Am**
Ah, ah, ah, ah, ah, ah, ah, ah, ah. Ah, ah, ah, ah, ah, ah, ah.

Outro

Am **G** **Am**
‖: Ah, ah, ah, ah, ah, ah, ah, ah, ah.
G **Am**
Ah, ah, ah, ah, ah, ah, ah. :‖ ***Repeat and fade***

Look So Fine, Feel So Low

Words and Music by
Paul Kelly and Maurice Frawley

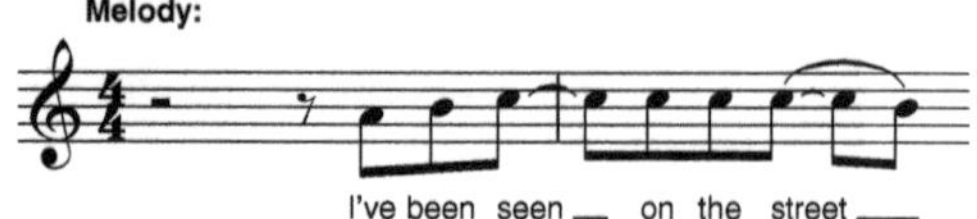

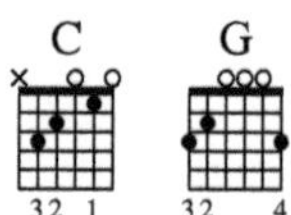

Intro

‖: N.C.(C) | (G) | (C) | (G) :‖
| (C) | (G) | (C) | (G) |
Ooh.
‖: C G | | C G | :‖

Verse 1

C G
I've been seen on the street
C G
Wearing brand new clothes.
C G
I guess I've ___ landed on my feet
C G
I'm a lucky guy I suppose.

Verse 2

C G
She tells me that ___ she loves me.
C G
She buys me things.
C G
She wants to take care of me,
C G
And all I gotta do is ___ sing, sing, sing, sing.

```
                C        G               C        G
Chorus 1          Well, I look so fine ___ but I feel so low.

                C        G               C        G
                  Yeah, I look so fine ___ but I feel so low.

                   C                    G
Verse 3         She takes me by the arm.

                   C              G
                She takes me all a - round.

                       C                          G
                And she knows all her friends are talking,

                      C                         G
                Saying, look what our good girls found.

                C             G
Verse 4           One thing ___ she's got on you,

                C          G
                  She's so easy to impress.

                C            G
                  When she asks me dumb questions,

                C              G
                All I gotta do is say yes, yes, yes, yes.
```

Chorus 2 *Repeat Chorus 1*

Guitar Solo ‖: C G | | C G | :‖

Outro-Chorus *Repeat Chorus 1 and fade*

The Name Game

Words and Music by
Lincoln Chase and Shirley Elliston

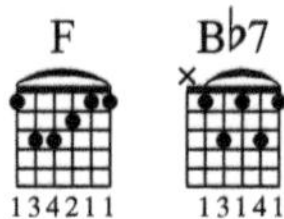


```
             F
*Intro*        The name game.

             F
*Chorus 1*     Shirley! Shirley, Shirley, bo-ber-ly, bo-na-na fan-na fo-fer-ley,
             B♭7              F
             Fee-fi mo-mer-ley.   Shirley!

             Lincoln! Lincoln, Lincoln, bo-bin-coln, bo-na-na fan-na fo-fin-coln,
             B♭7                F
             Fee-fi mo-min-coln.    Lincoln!
```

```
           F
Verse 1    Come on ev'rybody. I say now let's play a game.
                     B♭7                            F
           I betcha I can make a rhyme out of anybody's name.

           The first letter of the name, I treat it like it wasn't there.
                  B♭7                  F
           But a "B" or an "F," or an "M" will appear.

           And then I say "Bo" add a "B" then I say the name,

           Then "Bonana, fanna" and "fo."
                        B♭7
           And then I say the name again with an "F" very plain,
                   F
           Then a "fee-fi" and a "mo."
                        B♭7
           And then I say the name again with an "M" this time.
                        F
           And there isn't any name that I can't rhyme.

           F
Chorus 2   Arnold! Arnold, Arnold, bo-bar-nold, bo-na-na fan-na fo-far-nold,
           B♭7                F
           Fee-fi mo-mar-mold,    Arnold!
```

```
            F               B♭7
Verse 2       But if the first two letters are ever the same,
            F
            Drop them both, then say the name.

            Like Bob, Bob, drop the "B's" Bo-ob,

            Or Fred, Fred, drop the "F's" Fo-red,
              B♭7
            Or Mary, Mary, drop the "M's" Mo-ar-y.
            F
            That's the only rule that's contrary.

            Say "Bo" add a "B" now to Tony with a "B,"
                                        F
            Now "Bonana, fanna" and "fo."
                            B♭7
            And now you say the name again with an "F" very plain,
                      F
            Then "fee-fi" and a "mo."
                            B♭7
            And then you say the name again with an "M" this time.
                          F
            And there isn't any name that you can't rhyme.

            F
Chorus 3    Tony! Tony, Tony, bo-bo-ny, bo-na-na fan-na fo-fo-ny,
            B♭7                F
            Fee-fi mo-mo-ny.     Tony! Let's do Billy!

            Billy, Billy, bo-gil-ly, bo-na-na fan-na fo-fil-ly,
            B♭7               F
            Fee-fi mo-mil-ly.     Billy! Let's do Marsha!

            Marsha, Marsha, bo-bar-sha, bo-na-na fan-na fo-far-sha,
            B♭7                F
            Fee-fi mo-ar-sha.     Marsha! Little trick with Nick!

            Nick, Nick, bo-bick, bo-na-na fan-na fo-fick,
            B♭7              F
            Fee-fi mo-mick.     Nick! The name game.
```

Oye Como Va

Words and Music by
Tito Puente

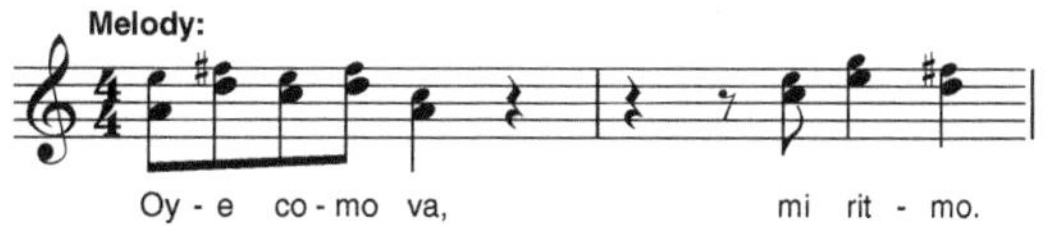

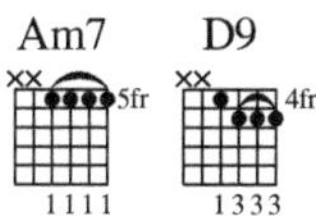

Intro	‖: **Am7** **D9** | :‖	***Play 8 times***
Verse 1	**Am7** **D9** ‖: Oye como va, mi ritmo. **Am7** **D9** Bueno pa gozar, mulata. :‖	
Guitar Solo 1	‖: **Am7** **D9** | :‖	***Play 10 times***
Interlude	‖: **Am7** **D9** | :‖	***Play 8 times***
Organ Solo	‖: **Am7** **D9** | :‖	***Play 11 times***
Verse 2	*Repeat Verse 1*	
Guitar Solo 2	‖: **Am7** **D9** | :‖	***Play 12 times***
Outro	| **Am7** | **D9** **Am7** | **D9** | **Am7** ‖ *Uhh!*	

Okie from Muskogee

Words and Music by
Merle Haggard and Roy Edward Burris

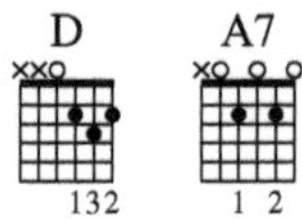

Verse 1

```
D
We don't smoke marijuana in Muskogee,
                                  A7
And we don't take our trips on L.S.D.

And we don't burn our draft cards down on Main Street,
                                D
But we like livin' right and being free.
```

Chorus 1

```
      D
And I'm proud to be an Okie from Muskogee;
                                       A7
A place where even squares can have a ball.

We still wave Ol' Glory down at the Court House,
                                         D
White lightning's still the biggest thrill of all.
```

Verse 2

D
We don't make a party out of loving,

A7
But we like holding hands and pitching woo.

We don't let our hair grow long and shaggy

D
Like the hippies out in San Francisco do.

Chorus 2 — ***Repeat Chorus 1***

Verse 3

D
Leather boots are still in style if a man needs footwear,

A7
Beads and Roman sandals won't be seen.

Football's still the roughest thing on campus,

D
And the kids here still respect the College Dean.

Chorus 3 — ***Repeat Chorus 1***

Paperback Writer

Words and Music by John Lennon
and Paul McCartney

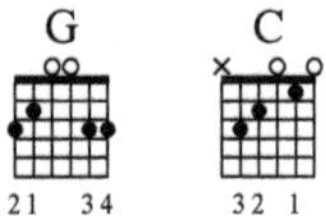

Intro

N.C.
Paperback writer... writer... writer.
| **G** | | | | |

Verse 1

G
Dear Sir or Madam, will you read my book?

It took me years to write, will you take a look?

It's based on a novel by a man named Lear,

And I need a job,

C
So I want to be a paperback writer,

G
Paperback writer.

```
                G
Verse 2         It's a dirty story of a dirty man,

                And his clinging wife who doesn't understand.

                His son is working for the Daily Mail.

                It's a steady job,
                                                C
                But he wants to be a paperback writer,
                          G
                Paperback writer.
                N.C.                                        G
                (Paperback writer, paperback writer.)

                G
Verse 3         It's a thousand pages, give or take a few.

                I'll be writing more in a week or two.

                I can make it longer if you like the style,

                I can change it 'round,
                                                C
                And I want to be a paperback writer,
                          G
                Paperback writer.
```

```
Verse 4      G
             If you really like it, you can have the rights.

             It could make a million for you overnight.

             If you must return it, you can send it here.

             But I need a break,
                                           C
             And I want to be a paperback writer,
                       G
             Paperback writer.
              N.C.                                    G
             (Paperback writer, paperback writer.)

                  G
Outro        ||: (Paperback writer, paperback writer.) :||  Repeat and fade
```

Pistol Packin' Mama

Words and Music by
Al Dexter

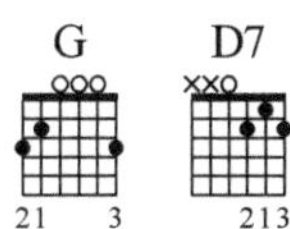

Verse 1

G … **D7**
Drinkin' beer in a cabaret, and was I havin' fun!

… **G**
Until one night she caught me right, and now I'm on the run.

Chorus 1

G … **D7**
Lay that pistol down, babe, lay that pistol down.

… **G**
Pistol Packin' Mama, lay that pistol down.

Verse 2

G … **D7**
She kicked out my windshield, she hit me over the head.

… **G**
She cussed and cried and said I lied, and wished that I was dead.

Chorus 2 *Repeat Chorus 1*

Verse 3

G … **D7**
Drinkin' beer in a cabaret, and dancin' with a blonde,

… **G**
Until one night she shot out the light, Bang! that blonde was gone.

Chorus 3 *Repeat Chorus 1*

Paradise

Words and Music by Helen Adu,
Stuart Matthewman, Andrew Hale
and Paul Denman

Melody:

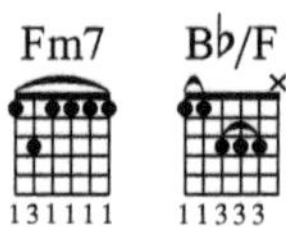

Intro | **Fm7** | **B♭/F** | **Fm7** | **B♭/F** |

Verse 1

```
                     Fm7
I'd wash the sand off the shore,
B♭/F                          Fm7
  Give you the world if it was mine.
B♭/F         Fm7              B♭/F  Fm7      B♭/F
  Blow you right to my door,          feels fine.
```

Chorus 1

```
Fm7      B♭/F         Fm7       B♭/F
Feels like you're mine, feels right, so fine.
Fm7       B♭/F                     Fm7  B♭/F  Fm7  B♭/F
I'm yours, you're mine like paradise.
```

Bridge

```
Fm7  B♭/F                          Fm7 B♭/F Fm7 B♭/F
          I'd give you the world if it was mine.

Fm7     B♭/F
Feels fine.

Fm7     B♭/F         Fm7
Feels like you're mine, I'm yours,

B♭/F               Fm7 B♭/F Fm7 B♭/F
So fine, like paradise.
```

Verse 2

Repeat Verse 1

Chorus 2

```
Fm7     B♭/F         Fm7       B♭/F
Feels like you're mine, feels right, so fine.

Fm7      B♭/F                   Fm7 B♭/F Fm7
I'm yours, you're mine like paradise.
```

Outro

```
   B♭/F  Fm7        B♭/F   Fm7
||: Ooh, what a life,    ooh, what a life.      :||

   B♭/F     Fm7
||: I wanna share my life,

          B♭/F
I wanna share my life with you.

          Fm7
I wanna share my life. :||
```
Repeat and fade

Planet Caravan

Words and Music by
Frank Iommi, John Osbourne,
William Ward and Terence Butler

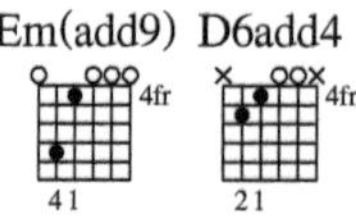

Intro

||: Em(add9) | D6add4 :||

Verse 1

Em(add9) D6add4 Em(add9)
We sail through endless skies,
D6add4 Em(add9) D6add4 Em(add9)
Stars shine like eyes, the black night sighs.
D6add4 Em(add9) D6add4 Em(add9)
The moon ___ in silver dreams,
D6add4 Em(add9) D6add4 Em(add9)
Falls down in peace, light of the night.
D6add4 Em(add9) D6add4 Em(add9)
The earth, ________ a purple blaze,
D6add4 Em(add9) D6add4 Em(add9) D6add4
A sapphire haze _______ in orbit al - ways.

Interlude

||: Em(add9) | D6add4 :||

Verse 2

Em(add9) D6add4 Em(add9)
While down below the trees,
D6add4 Em(add9) D6add4 Em(add9)
Bathing through breeze, silver starlight
D6add4 Em(add9) D6add4 Em(add9)
Breaks down from night. And so
D6add4 Em(add9) D6add4 Em(add9)
We pass on by the crimson night
D6add4 Em(add9) D6add4 Em(add9)
On great god Mars as we tra - vel
D6add4 Em(add9) D6add4
The universe.

Outro-Guitar Solo

||: Em(add9) | D6add4 :||

Pushin' Too Hard

Words and Music by
Sky Saxon

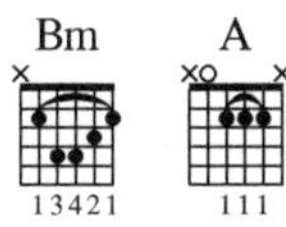

Intro ‖: Bm A | Bm A :‖

Chorus 1

```
          Bm                A       Bm           A
You're pushin' too hard, ___ uh, pushin' on me.
          Bm                A                Bm          A
You're pushin' too hard, ___ uh, what you want me to be?
          Bm                A            Bm          A
You're pushin' too hard ___ about the things you say.
          Bm                A         Bm          A
You're pushin' too hard ___ ev'ry night and day.
          Bm                A  Bm             A
You're pushin' too hard, ___ pushin' too hard
       Bm  A        Bm  A  Bm  A
On me. _____ (Too hard.)
```

Verse 1

```
        Bm A        Bm      A
Well, all I want is to just be free.

Bm          A             Bm     A
Live my life ___ the way I wanna be.

Bm        A        Bm             A
All I want ___ is to just to have fun.

Bm          A           Bm       A
Live my life ___ like it's just begun.
```

Chorus 2

```
                Bm                A   Bm            A
But you're pushin' too hard. ___ Pushin' too hard

           Bm A       Bm A Bm A Bm A
On me. _____ (Too hard.)
```

Organ Solo

```
||: Bm   A   | Bm   A   :||  Play 4 times
| Bm  A Bm  |      A Bm  |
| Bm    A   | Bm   A     |
```

Guitar Solo

```
||: Bm   A   | Bm   A   :||  Play 5 times
```

Verse 2

```
Bm            A             Bm      A
Better listen, girl, what I'm tellin' you.

     Bm          A      Bm           A
You better listen girl, or we are through.

     Bm              A       Bm           A
You better stop all ___ your foolin' around.

Bm             A        Bm           A
Stop your run - nin' all ___ over town.
```

Chorus 3

```
                 Bm                A   Bm            A
'Cause you're pushin' too hard. ___ Pushin' too hard

          Bm A      Bm A Bm A
On me. _____ (Too hard.)
```

Verse 3

```
     Bm    A           Bm        A
Well, I know there's a lotta fish in the sea.

Bm    A              Bm      A
I know some would uh, stay by me.

   Bm   A              Bm     A
So, if you don't think I'm gonna try,

   Bm               A      Bm       A
You better ask your - self the reason why.
```

Chorus 4

```
                 Bm                A   Bm            A
'Cause you're pushin' too hard, ___ pushin' too hard

          Bm A      Bm A Bm A
On me. _____ (Too hard.)

Bm               A   Bm           A
Pushin' too hard, ___ pushin' too hard,

Bm               A   Bm           A
Pushin' too hard, ___ pushin' too hard

          Bm A      Bm A Bm A
On me. _____ (Too hard.)
```

Outro

```
   Bm                A   Bm            A
‖: Pushin' too hard, ___ pushin' too hard. :‖ Repeat and fade
```

Rainy Day Woman

Words and Music by
Waylon Jennings

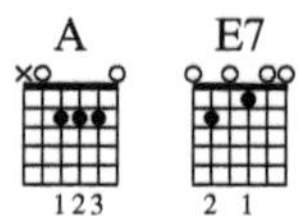

Intro

N.C. | A | | E7 | |
| | | A | |

Chorus 1

A   E7
Oh, rainy day woman, I've never seemed to see you

For the good times or the sunshine.

                                                            A
You have been a friend of mine, rainy day woman.

Verse

      A
That woman of mine she ain't happy

          E7
Till she finds somethin' wrong and someone to blame.

                                                                A
If it ain't one thing, it's another one on the way.

Woke up this mornin' to the sunshine.

E7
Sure as hell, looks just like rain.

                                                 A
I know where to go on a cloudy day.

Chorus 2   *Repeat Chorus 1*

Respect Yourself

Words and Music by
Mack Rice and Luther Ingram

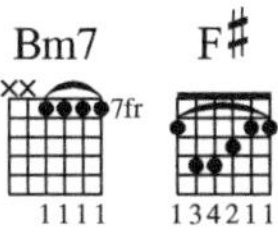

Verse 1

Bm7
Male: If you disrespect ev'rybody that you run in to,

How in the world do you think ev'rybody's s'posed to respect you?

If you don't give a heck about the man with the Bible in his hand y'all.

Just get out the way and let the gentleman do his thing.

You're the kind of gentleman that want ev'rything your way. Yeah.

Take the sheet off your face, boy, it's a brand-new day.

Chorus 1

Bm7
Respect yourself, respect yourself.

F♯
If you don't respect yourself,

Ain't nobody gonna give a good cahoot.

Bm7
Re - spect yourself, na, na, respect yourself.

Bm7

Interlude Da, da, da, da, da, da, da, da, da.

Da, da, da, da, da, da, da, da, da, da, da.

Yip, didle, le, didle, do, do.

Yip, didle, le, didle, do, do.

Yip, didle, le, didle, do, do,

Yip, didle, le, didle, do, do.

Bm7

Verse 2 *Female:* If you're walkin' 'round thinkin' that the world

Owes you something 'cause you're here. Ah.

You're goin' out the world backwards like you did

When you first came here, yeah.

Keep talkin' 'bout the president won't stop air pollution.

Put your hand on your mouth when you cough, that'll help the solution.

Oh, you curse around women though you don't even know their names, no.

And you're dumb enough to think

That'll make you a big old man, yeah, yeah.

Chorus 2

Bm7
'Spect yourself, oh, yeah. Respect yourself.

F#
If you don't respect yourself,

Ain't nobody gonna give a good cahoot.

Na, na, na, na, ah.

Outro

Bm7
‖: Re - spect yourself, respect yourself.

Respect yourself, respect yourself. :‖ ***Repeat and fade w/ vocal ad lib.***

Ramblin' Man

Words and Music by Hank Williams

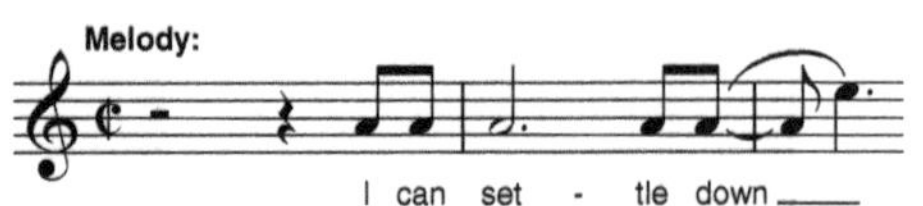

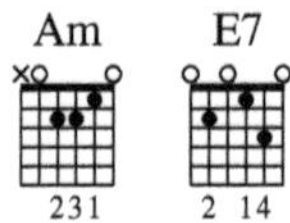

Intro |Am | | | |

Verse 1

```
   Am
I can settle down and be doin' just fine
          E7                              Am
'Til I hear ___ an old freight rollin' down the line.

Then I hurry straight home and pack.
      E7                          Am
And if I didn't go I b'lieve I'd blow my stack.

I love you, baby, but you gotta understand
         E7                               Am
When the Lord made me, He made a ramblin' man.
```

Verse 2

Am
Some folks might say that I'm no good,

E7 Am
That I wouldn't settle down if I could.

But when that open road starts to callin' me

E7 Am
There's somethin' o'er the hill that I gotta see.

Sometimes it's hard but you gotta understand

E7 Am
When the Lord made me, He made a ramblin' man.

Verse 3

Am
I love to see the town's a passin' by

E7 Am
And to ride these rails 'neath God's blue sky.

Let me travel this land from the mountains to the sea

E7 Am
'Cause that's the life I believe He meant for me.

And when I'm gone and at my grave you stand,

E7 Am
Just say God's ___ called home your ramblin' man.

Roadrunner

Words and Music by
Jonathan Richman

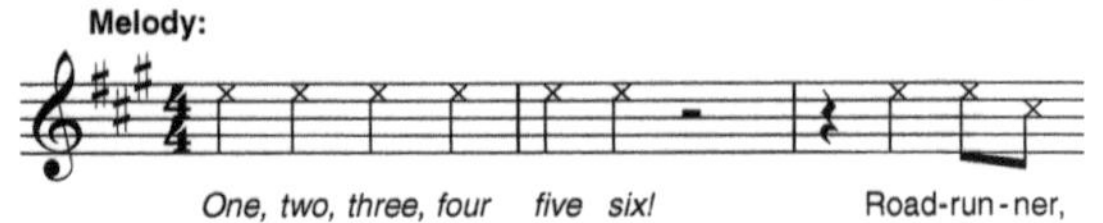

Melody:
One, two, three, four five six! Road-run-ner,

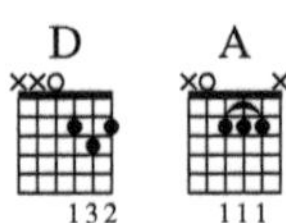

D
A
132
111

```
              N.C.                        D
*Intro*       One, two, three, four, five, six!

              A                          D
*Verse 1*       Roadrunner, roadrunner,
              A                           D
                Going faster miles an hour.
              A                                  D
                Gonna drive past the Stop & Shop,
              A                D
                With the radio on.
              A                               D
                I'm in love with Massachusetts,
              A                                   D
                And the neon when it's cold outside,
              A                                     D
                And the highway when it's late at night.
              A                D           A            D
                Got the radio on.   I'm like a roadrunner.
```

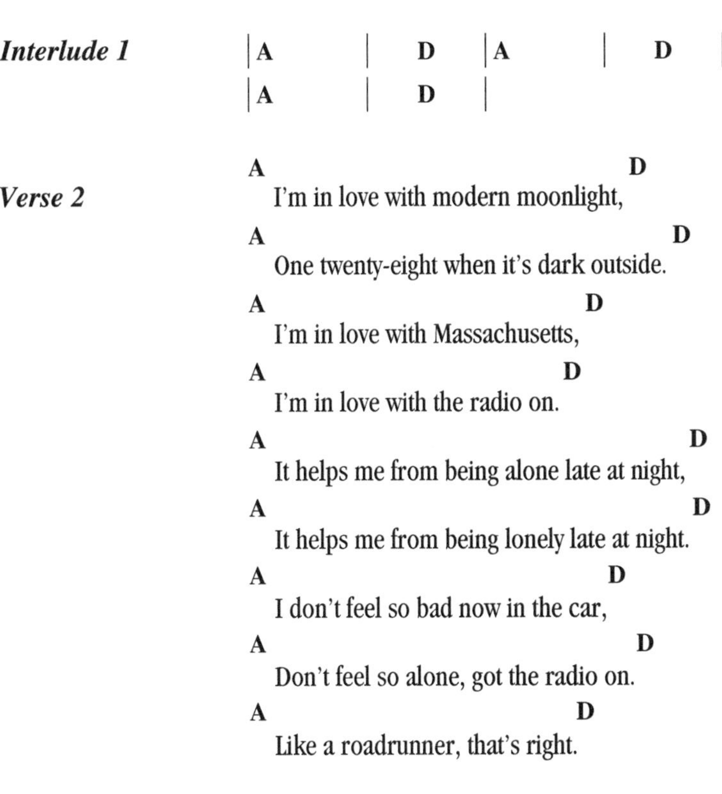

Interlude 1

| A | D | A | D |
| A | D |

Verse 2

A D
I'm in love with modern moonlight,
A D
One twenty-eight when it's dark outside.
A D
I'm in love with Massachusetts,
A D
I'm in love with the radio on.
A D
It helps me from being alone late at night,
A D
It helps me from being lonely late at night.
A D
I don't feel so bad now in the car,
A D
Don't feel so alone, got the radio on.
A D
Like a roadrunner, that's right.

Interlude 2 *Repeat Interlude 1*

```
             A                             D
Verse 3        I said hello to the spirit of 1956,
             A                              D
               Patient in the bushes next to '57.
             A                            D
               The highway is your girlfriend
             A                D
               As you go by quick,
             A                             D
              Suburban trees, suburban speed,
             A                       D
               And it smells like heaven.
             A                                            D
               And I say roadrunner once, roadrunner twice,
             A                          D
               I'm in love with rock 'n roll
             A                       D       A          D
               And I'll be out all night.   I'm a roadrunner.
```

Interlude 3 *Repeat Interlude 1*

```
             A                       D
Verse 4        Roadrunner, roadrunner,
             A                         D
               Going faster miles an hour.
             A                               D
               Gonna drive to the Stop & Shop
             A                       D
               With the radio on at night.
             A                                     D
               And be in love with modern moonlight,
             A                                D
               Be in love with modern rock 'n roll,
             A                                  D
               Modern girls and modern rock 'n roll,
             A                D
               Don't feel so alone.
             A                D        A
               Got the radio on,     like the roadrunner.
```

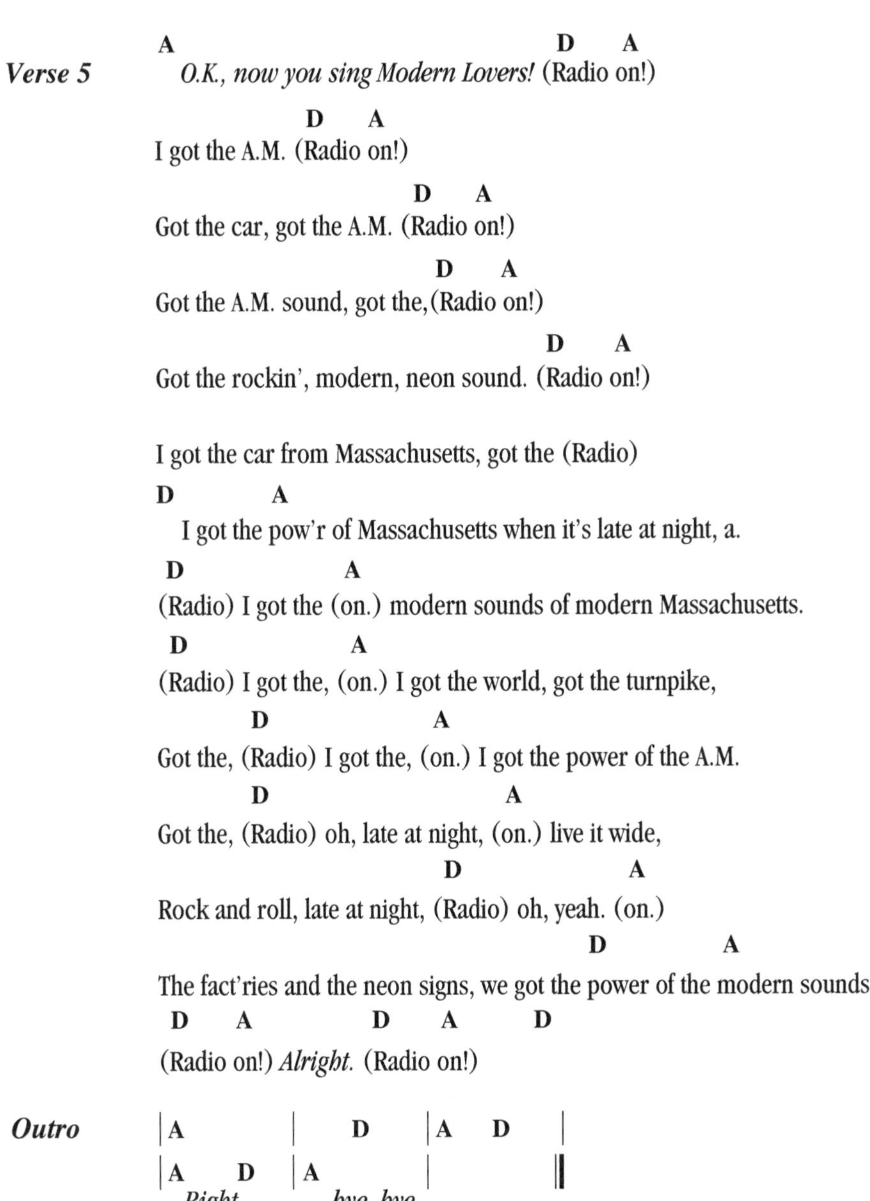

Verse 5

A D A
O.K., now you sing Modern Lovers! (Radio on!)

D A
I got the A.M. (Radio on!)

D A
Got the car, got the A.M. (Radio on!)

D A
Got the A.M. sound, got the,(Radio on!)

D A
Got the rockin', modern, neon sound. (Radio on!)

I got the car from Massachusetts, got the (Radio)

D A
I got the pow'r of Massachusetts when it's late at night, a.

D A
(Radio) I got the (on.) modern sounds of modern Massachusetts.

D A
(Radio) I got the, (on.) I got the world, got the turnpike,

D A
Got the, (Radio) I got the, (on.) I got the power of the A.M.

D A
Got the, (Radio) oh, late at night, (on.) live it wide,

D A
Rock and roll, late at night, (Radio) oh, yeah. (on.)

D A
The fact'ries and the neon signs, we got the power of the modern sounds.

D A D A D
(Radio on!) *Alright.* (Radio on!)

Outro

| **A** | **D** | **A D** |
| **A D** | **A** | ||
Right, bye, bye.

Rocking Pneumonia & Boogie Woogie Flu

Words and Music by
Huey P. Smith

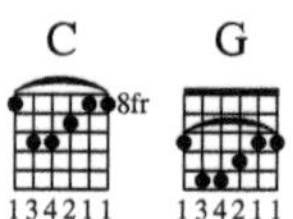

Intro

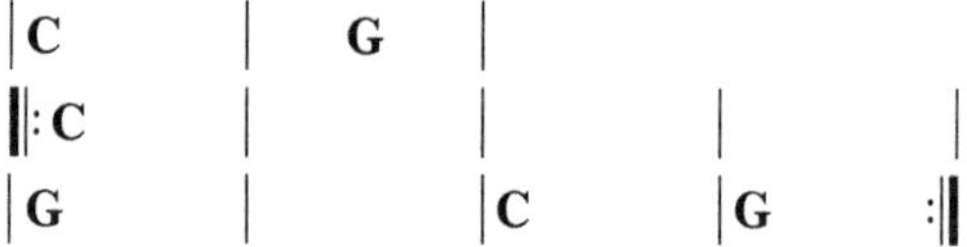

Verse 1

```
          C
I wanna jump but I'm afraid I'll fall.

I wanna holler but the joint's too small.
G
Young man rhythm's got a hold of me, too.
          C
I got the rockin' pneumonia and the boogie-woogie flu.
```

Verse 2

```
              C
Want some lovin', baby, that ain't all.

I wanna kiss her but she's way too tall.
G
Young man rhythm's got a hold of me, too.
          C
I got the rockin' pneumonia and the boogie-woogie flu.
```

Verse 3	**C** I wanna squeeze her but I'm way too low.
	I would be runnin' but my feet's too slow.
	G Young man rhythm's got a hold of me, too.
	C I got the rockin' pneumonia and the boogie-woogie flu.
Piano Solo	‖: **C** | | | | | **G** | | **C** | **G** :‖
Verse 4	*Repeat Verse 3*
Verse 5	**C** Baby, callin' now, I'm hurryin' home.
	I know she's leavin' 'cause I'm takin' too long.
	G Young man rhythm's got a hold of me, too.
	C I got the rockin' pneumonia and the boogie-woogie flu.
Outro-Guitar Solo	*Repeat Piano Solo and fade*

Show Biz Kids

Words and Music by
Walter Becker and Donald Fagen

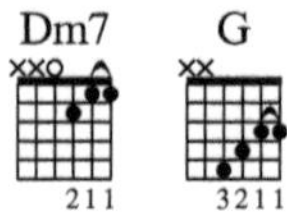

Intro | **Dm7 G Dm7** | **N.C.** |

```
         Dm7         G       Dm7   G       Dm7
      ||: Go to Las Wag - es, Las Wag - es,

                    G      Dm7
         Go to Las Wag - es.    :||  Play 4 times
```

```
                         Dm7
Chorus 1  ||: While the poor people sleepin' with the shade on the light,

          While the poor people sleepin' all the stars come out at night. :||
```

Interlude 1 | **Dm7 G Dm7** | **G Dm7** | **G Dm7** |

```
          Dm7
Verse 1      After closing time at the Guernsey Fair,

          I detect the El Supremo from the room at the top of the stairs.

          Well, I've been around the world, and I've been in the Washington Zoo.

          And in all my travels as the facts unravel, I found this to be true.
```

Chorus 2 *Repeat Chorus 1*

Interlude 2 *Repeat Interlude 1 (play 2 times)*

Verse 2

Dm7
They got the house on the corner with the rug inside.

They got the booze they need, all that money can buy.

They got the shapely bodies, they got the Steely Dan T-shirts,

And for the coup de grace they're outrageous.

Honey, let me tell you.

Chorus 3 *Repeat Chorus 1*

Interlude 3 *Repeat Interlude 1 (play 7 times)*

Bridge

Dm7
Show bus'ness kids makin' movies of themselves,

You know they don't give a fuck about anybody else.

You know you...

Outro w/ Chorus

Dm7 G Dm7
‖: Go to Las Wag - es,

G Dm7 G Dm7
Las Wag - es, go to Las Wag - es. :‖ ***Repeat and fade***

Solitude

Words and Music by Frank Iommi, William Ward, John Osbourne and Terence Butler

Melody:
My name it means noth-ing, _

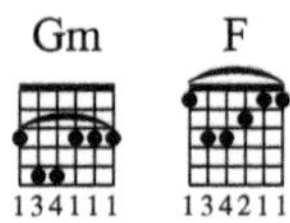
Gm
F
134111
134211

Intro ‖: Gm | F | Gm | F :‖ *Play 5 times*

Verse 1

```
    Gm          F                    Gm F Gm F
My name it means nothing, my fortune is less.
    Gm     F                      Gm F Gm F
My future is shrouded in dark wilder - ness.
Gm         F                     Gm F Gm F
Sunshine is far away, clouds linger on.
Gm          F                     G
Ev'rything I ___ possessed, now they are gone.
F          Gm  F         Gm F Gm F
   They are gone.   They are gone.
```

Interlude 1 ‖: Gm | F | Gm | F :‖ *Play 3 times*

```
              Gm           F                        Gm  F  Gm  F
Verse 2       Oh, where can I go to and what can I do?

              Gm           F                               Gm  F  Gm  F
              Nothing can please me, only thoughts are of you.

              Gm      F                                 Gm  F  Gm  F
              You just laughed when I begged you to stay.

              Gm               F                          Gm
              I've not stopped crying since you went a - way.

              F                  Gm   F               Gm  F  Gm  F
                 You went a - way.     You went a - way.

Guitar Solo   ||: Gm     | F       |         | Gm     :||  Play 4 times
              | F        | Gm      | F       |

                           Gm      F
Verse 3       The world ___ is a lonely place,

                                Gm  F  Gm  F
              You're on your own.

              Gm          F                          Gm  F  Gm  F
              Guess I will go home, sit down and moan.

              Gm          F                     Gm  F  Gm  F
              Crying and thinking is all that I do.

              Gm              F                       Gm  F    Gm
              Memories I ___ have remind me of you,      of you,

              F     Gm  F  Gm  F  Gm  F
                 Of you.

Outro         ||: Gm     | F       |         |
              | Gm       | F       | Gm      | F      :||  Repeat and fade
```

Something in the Way

Words and Music by
Kurt Cobain

Drop D tuning, down 1/2 step:
(low to high) D♭-A♭-D♭-G♭-B♭-E♭

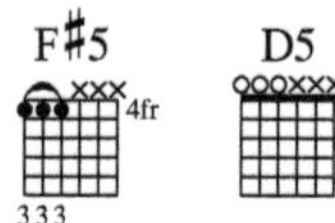


```
Intro      ||: F#5  D5   | F#5  D5   :||

           F#5                     D5  F#5                   D5
Verse 1    Underneath the bridge, ___ tarp has sprung a leak.
                   F#5                   D5       F#5              D5
           And the animals I've trapped ___ have all become my pets.
                   F#5                D5          F#5                     D5
           And I'm living off of grass ___ and the drippings from the ceil - ing.
           F#5                  D5               F#5                D5
           It's okay to eat fish ___ 'cause they don't have any feel - ings.

              F#5                   D5   F#5  D5
Chorus 1   ||: Something in the way. ___ Mm.
           F#5                  D5       F#5  D5
           Something in the way, ___ yeah. Mm.      :||  Play 3 times

Verse 2    Repeat Verse 1

              F#5                   D5   F#5  D5
Chorus 2   ||: Something in the way. ___ Mm.
           F#5                  D5       F#5  D5
           Something in the way, ___ yeah. Mm.      :||  Play 4 times
```

What I Got

Words and Music by Brad Nowell,
Eric Wilson, Floyd Gaugh and
Lindon Roberts

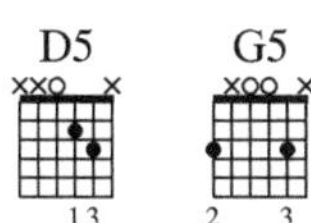

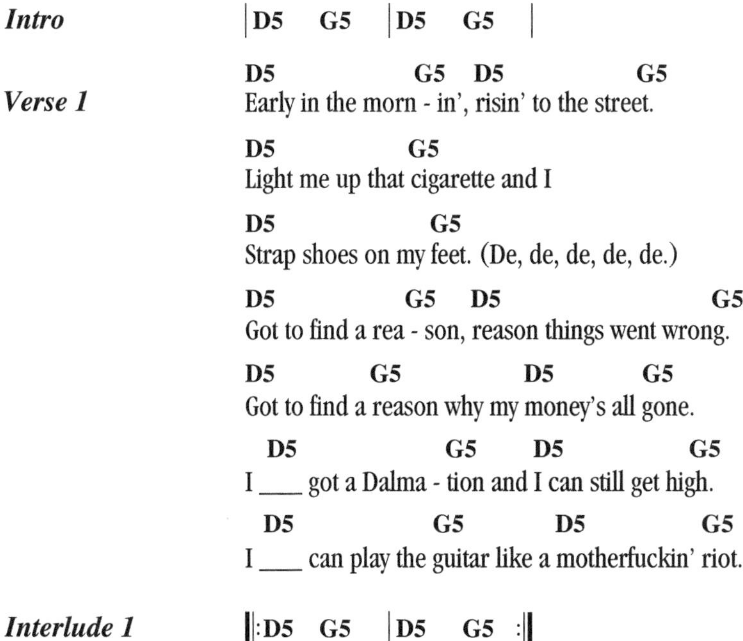

Intro

| D5 G5 | D5 G5 |

Verse 1

```
D5                 G5  D5              G5
Early in the morn - in', risin' to the street.
D5               G5
Light me up that cigarette and I
D5                   G5
Strap shoes on my feet. (De, de, de, de, de.)
D5               G5  D5                   G5
Got to find a rea - son, reason things went wrong.
D5          G5          D5          G5
Got to find a reason why my money's all gone.
  D5               G5     D5           G5
I ___ got a Dalma - tion and I can still get high.
  D5              G5         D5           G5
I ___ can play the guitar like a motherfuckin' riot.
```

Interlude 1

||: D5 G5 | D5 G5 :||

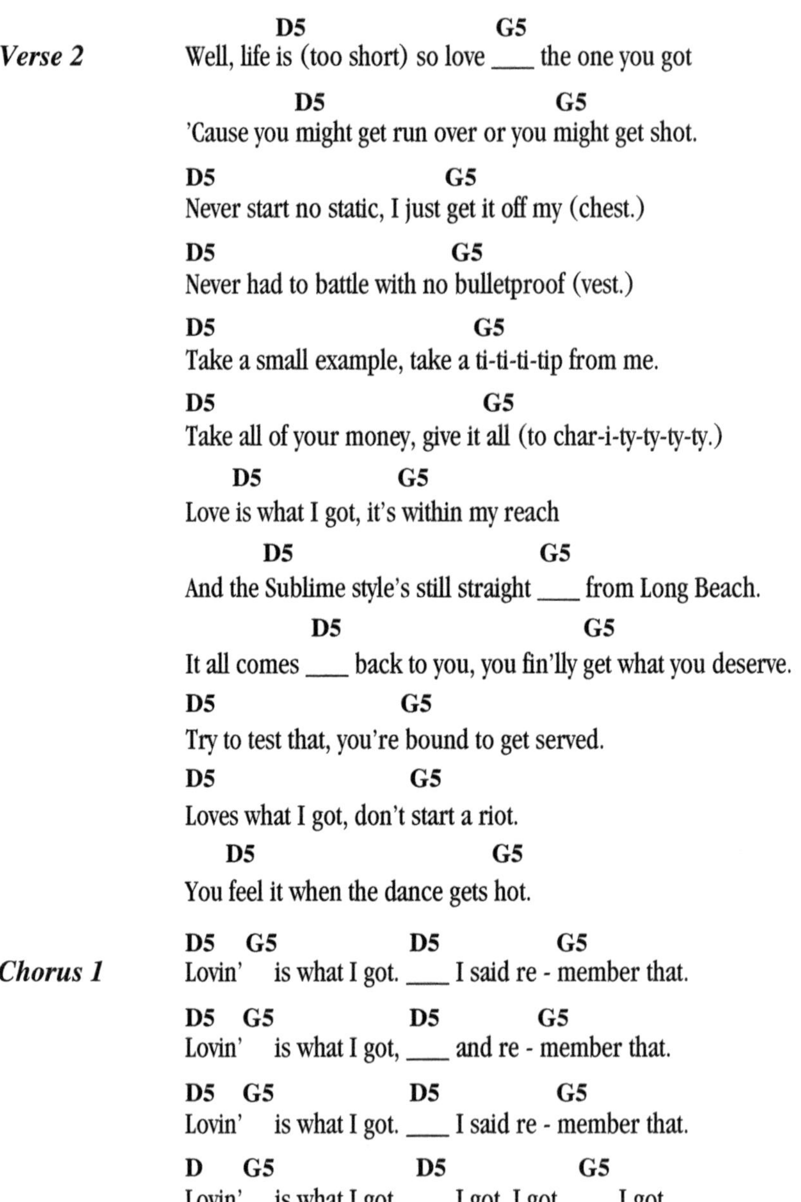

Verse 2

D5 G5
Well, life is (too short) so love ___ the one you got

D5 G5
'Cause you might get run over or you might get shot.

D5 G5
Never start no static, I just get it off my (chest.)

D5 G5
Never had to battle with no bulletproof (vest.)

D5 G5
Take a small example, take a ti-ti-ti-tip from me.

D5 G5
Take all of your money, give it all (to char-i-ty-ty-ty-ty.)

D5 G5
Love is what I got, it's within my reach

D5 G5
And the Sublime style's still straight ___ from Long Beach.

D5 G5
It all comes ___ back to you, you fin'lly get what you deserve.

D5 G5
Try to test that, you're bound to get served.

D5 G5
Loves what I got, don't start a riot.

D5 G5
You feel it when the dance gets hot.

Chorus 1

D5 G5 D5 G5
Lovin' is what I got. ___ I said re - member that.

D5 G5 D5 G5
Lovin' is what I got, ___ and re - member that.

D5 G5 D5 G5
Lovin' is what I got. ___ I said re - member that.

D G5 D5 G5
Lovin' is what I got, ___ I got, I got, ___ I got.

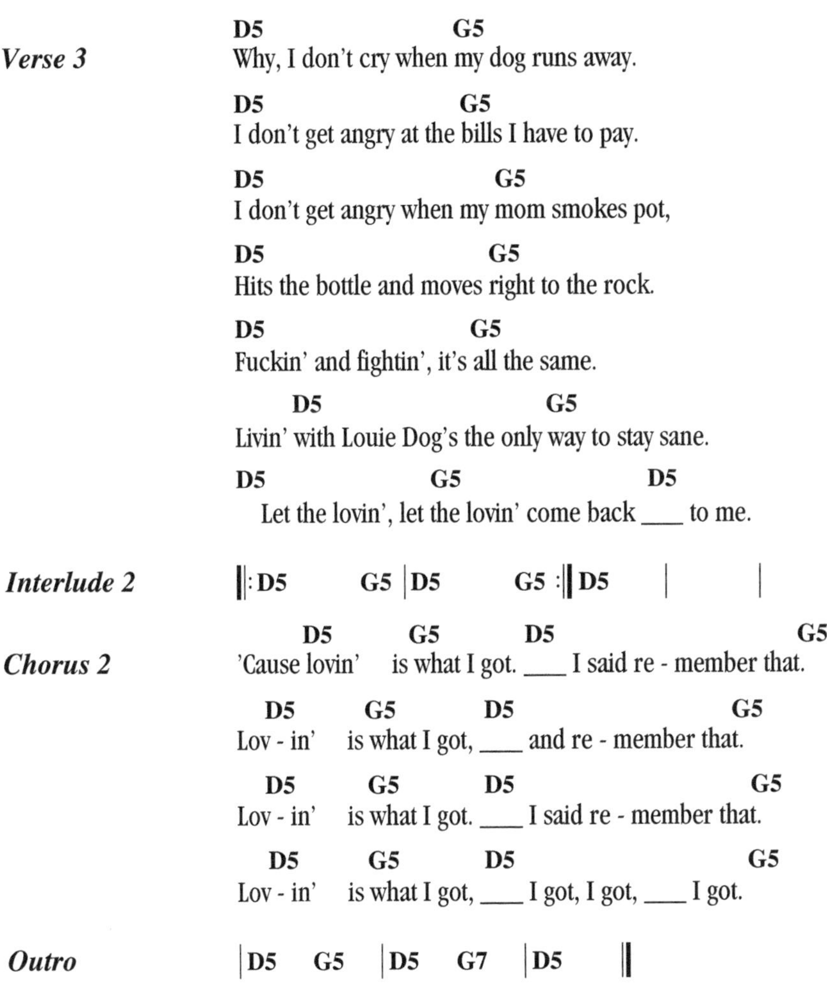

Verse 3

D5 G5
Why, I don't cry when my dog runs away.

D5 G5
I don't get angry at the bills I have to pay.

D5 G5
I don't get angry when my mom smokes pot,

D5 G5
Hits the bottle and moves right to the rock.

D5 G5
Fuckin' and fightin', it's all the same.

D5 G5
Livin' with Louie Dog's the only way to stay sane.

D5 G5 D5
Let the lovin', let the lovin' come back ___ to me.

Interlude 2

‖: D5 G5 | D5 G5 :‖ D5 | |

Chorus 2

D5 G5 D5 G5
'Cause lovin' is what I got. ___ I said re - member that.

D5 G5 D5 G5
Lov - in' is what I got, ___ and re - member that.

D5 G5 D5 G5
Lov - in' is what I got. ___ I said re - member that.

D5 G5 D5 G5
Lov - in' is what I got, ___ I got, I got, ___ I got.

Outro

| D5 G5 | D5 G7 | D5 ‖

Take Me Back to Tulsa

Words by Tommy Duncan
Music by Bob Wills

Melody:

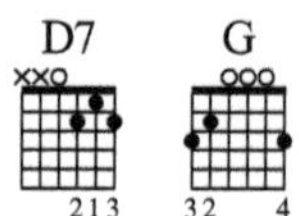

Intro ‖: D7 | | | G :‖ *Play 3 times*

Verse 1

```
G                                                    D7
Where's that gal with the red dress on? Some folks call her Dinah.
                                           G
Stole my heart away from me, way down in Louisi - ana.
```

Chorus 1

```
G                               D7
Take me back to Tulsa, I'm too young to marry.
                                G
Take me back to Tulsa, I'm too young to marry.
```

Interlude 1 *Repeat Intro (play 2 times)*

Verse 2

```
G                                             D7
Little bee sucks the blossom, the big bee gets the honey.
                                                G
The darkey raises cotton, the white man gets the mon - ey.
```

Chorus 2 *Repeat Chorus 1*

Interlude 2 *Repeat Intro (play 2 times)*

```
             G                                   D7
Verse 3      Oh, walk and talk Susie, walk and talk Susie.
                                                  G
             Oh, walk and talk Susie, walk and talk Susie.
```

Chorus 3 *Repeat Chorus 1*

Interlude 3 *Repeat Intro (play 2 times)*

```
             G                                          D7
Verse 4      We always wear a great big smile, we never do look sour.
                                                     G
             Travel all o'er the country, playing by the hour.
```

Chorus 4 *Repeat Chorus 1*

Interlude 4 *Repeat Intro (play 3 times)*

```
             G                                     D7
Chorus 5     Take me back to Tulsa, I'm too young to marry.
                                                   G
             Take me back to Tulsa, I'm too young to wed thee.
```

That's the Way (I Like It)

Words and Music by
Harry Wayne Casey and Richard Finch

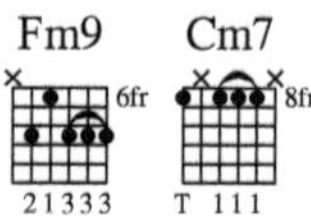

Intro

Fm9
‖: (Do, do, do, do, do, do, do, do, do.) :‖ *Play 4 times*

Chorus 1

Cm7
‖: That's the way, uh-huh, uh-huh,

I like it, uh-huh, uh-huh. :‖ *Play 4 times*

Verse 1

Fm9
When you take me by the hand,

Tell me I need your lovin' man,

When you give me all your love and do it, babe,

The very best you can, oh…

Chorus 2 *Repeat Chorus 1*

Verse 2	**Fm9** When I get to be in your arms, When we're all, all alone, When you whisper sweet in my ear, When you turn, turn me on, oh...
Interlude 1	‖: **Fm9** | | Babe, oh, babe. | | | *(That's the way, uh-huh. That's the way, uh-huh.* | | :‖ *That's the way, uh-huh. That's the way, uh-huh.)*
Chorus 3	*Repeat Chorus 1*
Interlude 2	*Repeat Intro*
Outro-Chorus	*Repeat Chorus 1 and fade*

Tomorrow Never Knows

Words and Music by John Lennon
and Paul McCartney

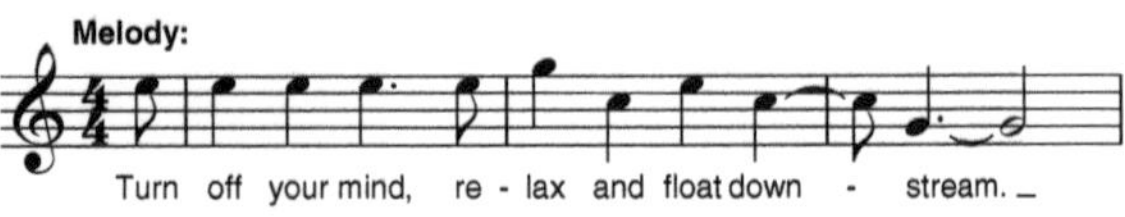

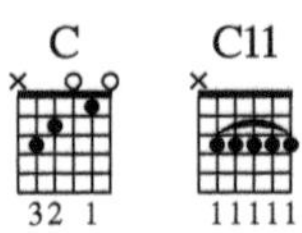

Intro | C | | | |

Verse 1

C
Turn off your mind,

Relax and float downstream.

C11 C
It is not dying, it is not dying.

Verse 2

C
Lay down all thought,

Surrender to the void.

C11 C
It is shining, it is shining.

Verse 3

C
That you may see

The meaning of within.

C11 C
It is being, it is being.

Solo ‖: C | | | :‖

Verse 4

```
C
That love is all

And love is everyone.
    C11          C
It is knowing, it is knowing.
```

Verse 5

```
C
That ignorance and hate

May mourn the dead.
       C11          C
It is be-lieving, it is be-lieving.
```

Verse 6

```
C
But listen to the

Color of your dreams.
       C11          C
It is not living, it is not living.
```

Verse 7

```
   C
Or play the game existence to the end.
         C11              C
Of the be-ginning, of the be-ginning.
         C11              C
Of the be-ginning, of the be-ginning.
         C11              C
Of the be-ginning, of the be-ginning.
         C11    C
Of the be-ginning.
```

Tulsa Time

Words and Music by
Danny Flowers

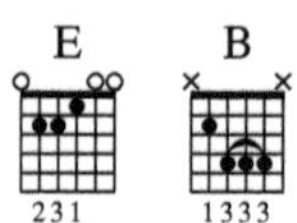

Intro | E | |

Verse 1

E
I ___ left Oklahoma drivin' in a Pontiac,

B
Just about to lose my mind.

I was goin' to Arizona, maybe on to California

E
Where the people all live so fine.

My baby said I's crazy, my Momma called me lazy,

B
I was goin' to show 'em all this time,

'Cause you know I ain't no foolin', I don't need no more schoolin',

E
I was born to just walk the line.

Chorus 1

E **B**
Livin' on Tulsa time. Livin' on Tulsa time.

Well, you know I been thru it when I set my watch back to it,

E
Livin' on Tulsa time.

Dobro Solo | E | | | B |
| | | | E |

Verse 2

E
Well, there I was in Hollywood wishin' I was doin' good,

B
Talkin' on the telephone line.

But they don't need me in the movies and nobody sings my songs,

E
Guess I'm just a-wastin' time.

Well, then I got to thinkin', man, I'm really sinkin'

B
And I really had a flash this time.

I had no business leavin' and nobody would be grievin'

E
If I went on back to Tulsa time.

Chorus 2

E B
‖: Livin'on Tulsa time. Livin' on Tulsa time.

Gonna set my watch back to it, 'cause you know I've been thru it,

E
Livin' on Tulsa time. :‖

Outro *Repeat Dobro Solo and fade*

Use Me

Words and Music by
Bill Withers

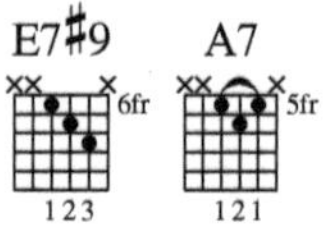

Intro ‖: E7♯9 | A7 :‖

Verse 1

```
                E7♯9 A7                    E7♯9 A
My friends ___       feel it's their appointed duty.
                        E7♯9  A7                    E7♯9      A7
They keep tryin' to tell me   all you want to do is use ___ me.
           E7♯9   A7                   E7♯9 A7
But my answer     to all that "use me" stuff
    N.C.
Is that I want to spread the news that if it feels this good gettin' used
                                                       E7♯9 A7
Oh, you just keep on usin' me until you use me up.
                     E7♯9 A7
Until you use me up.
```

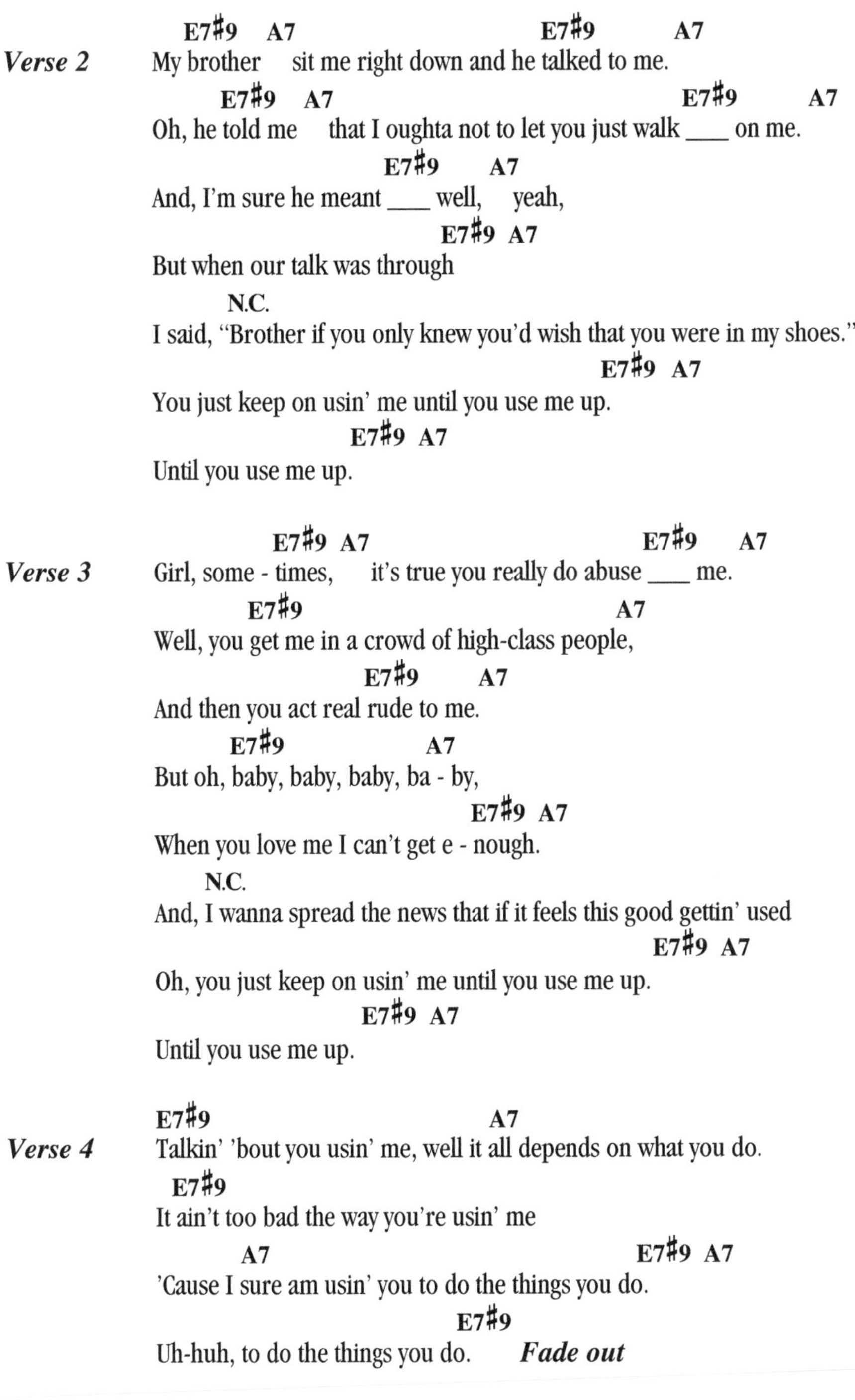

Verse 2

E7#9 A7 E7#9 A7
My brother sit me right down and he talked to me.
E7#9 A7 E7#9 A7
Oh, he told me that I oughta not to let you just walk ___ on me.
E7#9 A7
And, I'm sure he meant ___ well, yeah,
E7#9 A7
But when our talk was through
N.C.
I said, "Brother if you only knew you'd wish that you were in my shoes."
E7#9 A7
You just keep on usin' me until you use me up.
E7#9 A7
Until you use me up.

Verse 3

E7#9 A7 E7#9 A7
Girl, some - times, it's true you really do abuse ___ me.
E7#9 A7
Well, you get me in a crowd of high-class people,
E7#9 A7
And then you act real rude to me.
E7#9 A7
But oh, baby, baby, baby, ba - by,
E7#9 A7
When you love me I can't get e - nough.
N.C.
And, I wanna spread the news that if it feels this good gettin' used
E7#9 A7
Oh, you just keep on usin' me until you use me up.
E7#9 A7
Until you use me up.

Verse 4

E7#9 A7
Talkin' 'bout you usin' me, well it all depends on what you do.
E7#9
It ain't too bad the way you're usin' me
A7 E7#9 A7
'Cause I sure am usin' you to do the things you do.
E7#9
Uh-huh, to do the things you do. ***Fade out***

Waltz Across Texas

Words and Music by
Talmadge Tubb

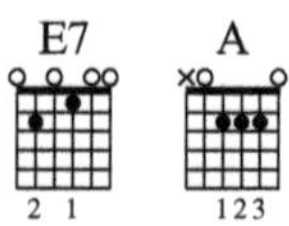

Intro

N.C. | E7 | | A | | E7 |

Verse 1

```
      A                         E7
When we dance together, my world's in the skies.
                                 A
It's a fairyland tale that's come true,
E7        A                          E7
And when you look at me with those stars in your eyes,
                                 A     E7
I could waltz across Texas with you.
```

Chorus 1

```
A                         E7
Waltz across Texas with you in my arms,
                          A
Waltz across Texas with you.
E7    A                    E7
Like a storybook ending, I'm lost in your charms,
                                     A     E7
And I could waltz across Texas with you.
```

Instrumental *Repeat Verse 1*

```
          A                                E7
Verse 2   My heartaches and troubles are just up and gone
                                         A
          The moment that you come in view.
          E7       A                                 E7
          And with your hand in mine, dear, I could dance on and on,
                                                A     E7
          And I could waltz across Texas with you.

          A                        E7
Chorus 2  Waltz across Texas with you in my arms,
                                    A
          Waltz across Texas with you.
          E7     A                       E7
          Like a storybook ending, I'm lost in your charms,
                                                A
          And I could waltz across Texas with you.
```

Whole Lotta Love

Words and Music by Jimmy Page,
Robert Plant, John Paul Jones,
John Bonham and Willie Dixon

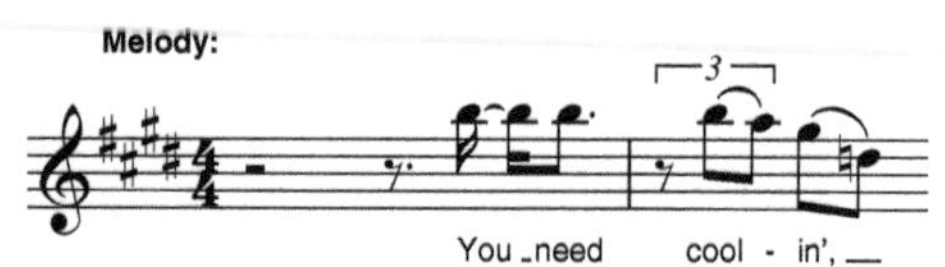

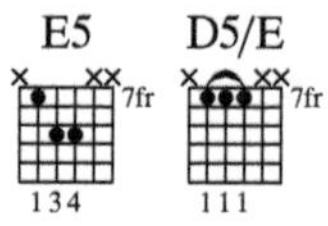

Intro N.C. | E5 | N.C. | E5 |

Verse 1

```
E5  N.C.       E5   N.C.              E5
    You need coolin',   baby, I'm not foolin',

N.C.          E5       N.C.       E5
I'm gonna send you     back to schoolin'.

N.C.  E5               N.C.  E5                    N.C.
  Uh, way down inside,         uh, honey you need it,

E5                             N.C.  E5                          N.C.
  I'm gonna give you my love,          I'm gonna give you my love.
```

Chorus 1

```
E5  D5/E                E5
Oh,    want a whole lotta love,

D5/E                  E5
  Want a whole lotta love,

D5/E                  E5
  Want a whole lotta love,

D5/E                  E5
  Want a whole lotta love.
```

Verse 2

```
N.C.               E5             N.C.                  E5
  You've been ___ learnin' and, baby, I've been ___ learnin',

N.C.        E5                    N.C.      E5        N.C.
  All them     good times, baby, baby, I've been yearnin'.

E5                       N.C.  E5                    N.C.
  Uh, way, way down inside,    uh, honey you need it,

E5                            N.C.  E5                              N.C.
  I'm gonna give you my love,    uh,   I'm gonna give you my love, uh.
```

Chorus 2

```
E5  D5/E            E5
Oh,     whole lotta love,

D5/E                   E5
   Want a whole lotta love,

D5/E                   E5
   Want a whole lotta love,

D5/E                        E5
   Want a whole lotta love. ___ I don't want more.
```

Interlude 1 ‖: N.C. :‖ ***Play 36 times***

Guitar Solo ‖: **E5** N.C. :‖ ***Play 6 times***

Verse 3

```
                 E5          N.C.       E5          N.C.
You've been ___ coolin',     baby, I been droolin',

E5                      N.C.        E5          N.C.
All the good times, ba - by, I been     misusin'.

E5                         N.C.  E5                            N.C.
   Uh, way, way down in - side,    I wanna give you my love,

E5                                          N.C.
   I'm gonna give you ev'ry inch of my ___ love,

E5                               N.C.  E5      N.C.          N.C.
   I'm gonna give you my love. ___     Yeah,     alright, let's go!
```

Chorus 3

```
  E5  D5/E
‖:        Want a whole lotta love,

E5  D5/E
          Want a whole lotta love. :‖
```

Interlude 2

```
E5  N.C.
     Way down inside, woman, you need, yeah, love.
```

Outro ‖: **E5** N.C. | **E5** N.C. :‖ ***Repeat and fade w/ vocal ad lib.***

You Never Can Tell

Words and Music by
Chuck Berry

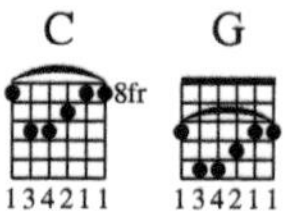

Intro | N.C.(C) | (G) |

Verse 1

(C) It was a teenage wedding and the old folks wished them well.

You could see that Pierre did truly love the Mademoiselle. (G)

And now the young monsieur and madame have rung the chapel bell.

"C'est la vie," say the old folks, it goes to show you never can tell. (C)

Verse 2

(C) They furnished off an apartment with a two room Roebuck sale.

The coolerator was crammed with TV dinners and ginger ale. (G)

But when Pierre found work the little money comin' worked out well.

"C'est la vie," say the old folks, it goes to show you never can tell. (C)

```
                    C
Verse 3       They had a hi-fi phono, boy, did they let it blast.
                                                        G
              Seven-hundred little records, all rock, rhythm and jazz.

              But when the sun went down the rapid tempo of the music fell.
                                                                 C
              "C'est la vie," say the old folks, it goes to show you never can tell.

                      C
Verse 4       They bought a souped-up jitney 'twas a cheery red '53.
                                                           G
              They drove it down to Orleans to celebrate the anniversary.

              It was there where Pierre was wedded to the lovely Mademoiselle.
                                                                 C
              "C'est la vie," say the old folks, it goes to show you never can tell.
```

Piano Solo 1 *Repeat Verse 1 (Instrumental)*

```
                    C
Verse 5       They had a teenage wedding and the old folks wished them well.
                                                          G
              You could see that Pierre did truly love the Mademoiselle.

              And now the young monsieur and madame have rung the chapel bell.
                                                                 C
              "C'est la vie," say the old folks, it goes to show you never can tell.
```

Outro-
Piano Solo *Repeat Piano Solo 1 and fade*

When Love Comes to Town

Words by Bono and The Edge
Music by U2

Melody:

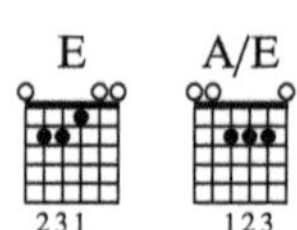

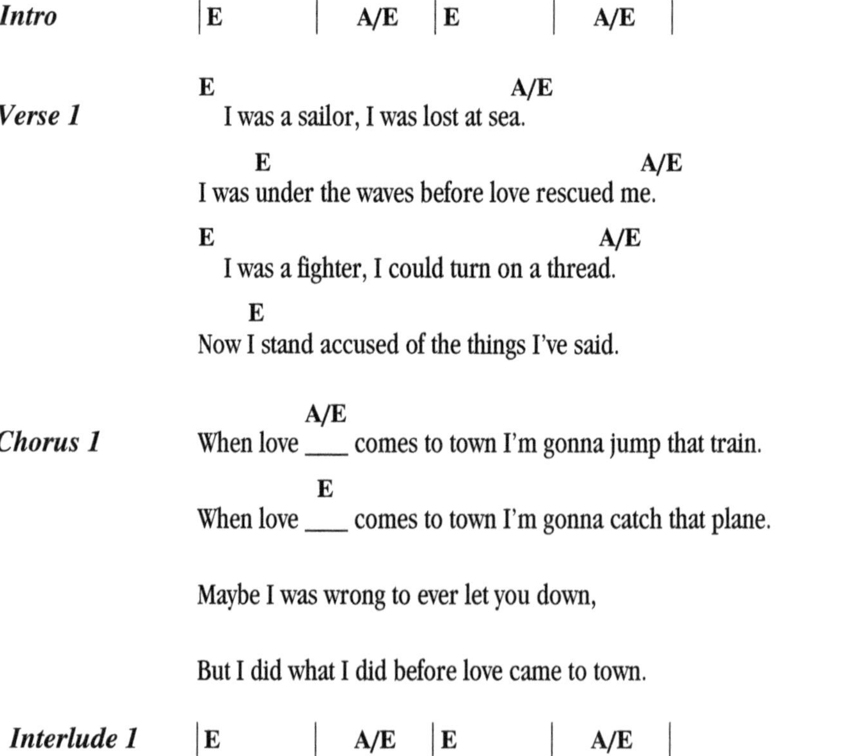

Intro | E | A/E | E | A/E |

Verse 1

```
E                          A/E
   I was a sailor, I was lost at sea.
     E                                A/E
I was under the waves before love rescued me.
E                                A/E
   I was a fighter, I could turn on a thread.
     E
Now I stand accused of the things I've said.
```

Chorus 1

```
          A/E
When love ___ comes to town I'm gonna jump that train.
          E
When love ___ comes to town I'm gonna catch that plane.

Maybe I was wrong to ever let you down,

But I did what I did before love came to town.
```

Interlude 1 | E | A/E | E | A/E |

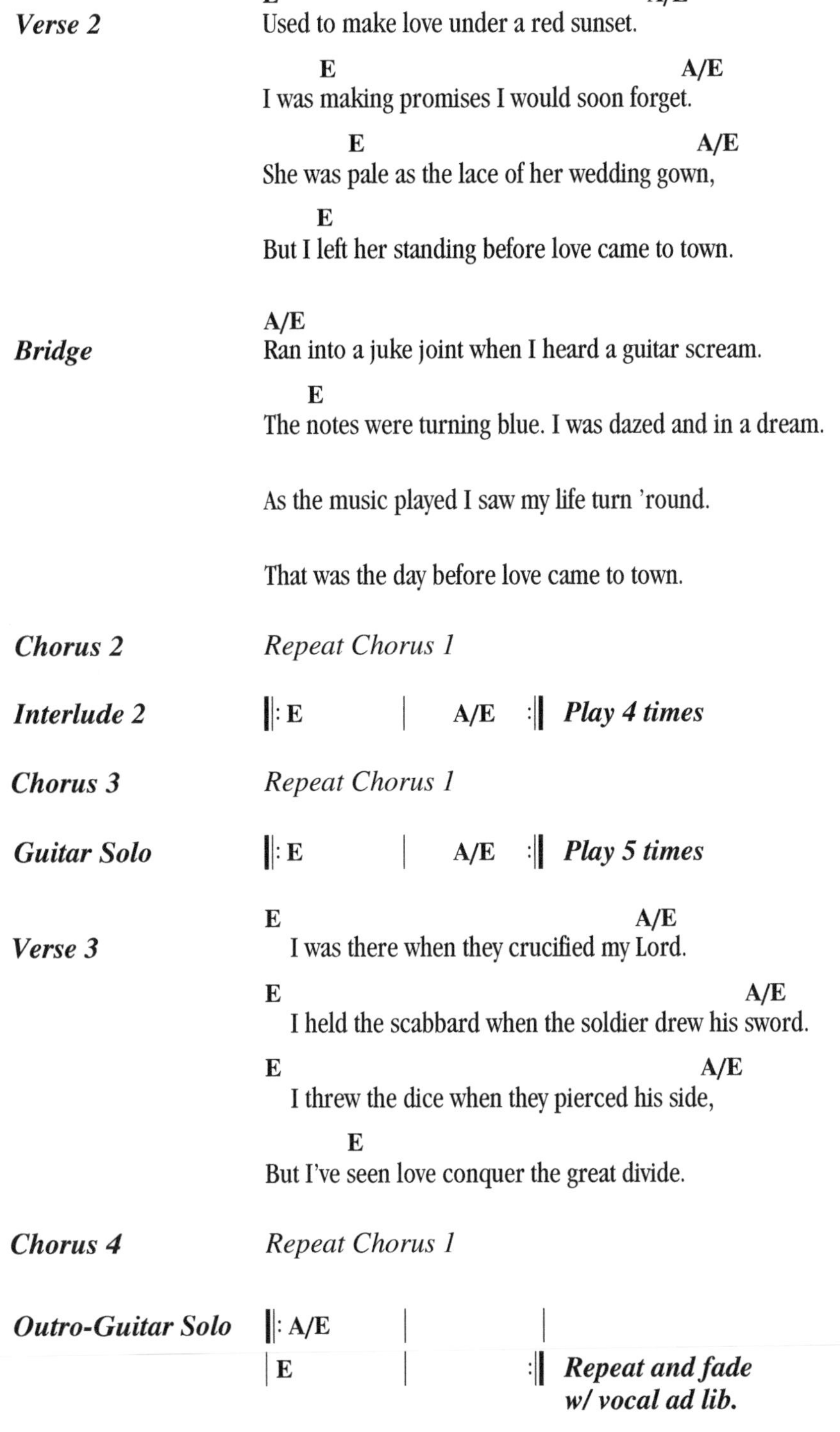

Verse 2

E **A/E**
Used to make love under a red sunset.

E **A/E**
I was making promises I would soon forget.

E **A/E**
She was pale as the lace of her wedding gown,

E
But I left her standing before love came to town.

Bridge

A/E
Ran into a juke joint when I heard a guitar scream.

E
The notes were turning blue. I was dazed and in a dream.

As the music played I saw my life turn 'round.

That was the day before love came to town.

Chorus 2 *Repeat Chorus 1*

Interlude 2 ||: **E** | **A/E** :|| ***Play 4 times***

Chorus 3 *Repeat Chorus 1*

Guitar Solo ||: **E** | **A/E** :|| ***Play 5 times***

Verse 3

E **A/E**
I was there when they crucified my Lord.

E **A/E**
I held the scabbard when the soldier drew his sword.

E **A/E**
I threw the dice when they pierced his side,

E
But I've seen love conquer the great divide.

Chorus 4 *Repeat Chorus 1*

Outro-Guitar Solo ||: **A/E** | |
| **E** | :|| ***Repeat and fade w/ vocal ad lib.***